Fireside

FLYING PIES of PRAISE

"Prosperity Pie is another rich offering—wise, relaxing, and sorely needed!" —Mimi Kennedy, "Abby," Dharma and Greg

"SARK is the real thing—wonderfully warm, tremendously inspiring, and refreshingly down-to-earth." —Cheri Huber, author of Suffering is Optional

"I love that SARK wrote this book . . . her entire body and soul and heart exude prosperity and abundance." —Leslie Bruhn, CPA

OTHER BOOKS BY SARK

A creative companion
HOW TO FREE YOUR CREATIVE SPIRIT
BY SARK

inspiration SANDWICH
STORIES TO INSPIRE OUR CREATIVE FREEDOM
BY SARK

LIVING JUICY
DAILY MORSELS FOR YOUR CREATIVE SOUL
BY SARK

THE MAGIC COTTAGE ADDRESS BOOK
BY SARK

SARK'S JOURNAL AND PLAY! BOOK
A PLACE TO DREAM WHILE AWAKE
BY SARK

NATIONAL BESTSELLER
Succulent Wild Woman
Dancing with your Wonder-full self!
BY SARK

THE BODACIOUS BOOK of Succulence
DARING TO LIVE YOUR SUCCULENT WILD LIFE!
BY SARK

THE ULTIMATE NAP BOOK
CHANGE YOUR LIFE WITHOUT GETTING OUT OF BED
BY SARK

Transformation SOUP
BY SARK
HEALING for the Splendidly imperfect

EAT MANGOES NAKED BY SARK
FINDING PLEASURE everywhere and DANCING with the PITS!

prosperity pie

HOW TO reLAX ABOUT MONEY and everyThing else

BY SARK

A Fireside BOOK

PUBLISHed BY SIMON & Schuster

new YORK LonDon Toronto SYDneY SINGAPORE

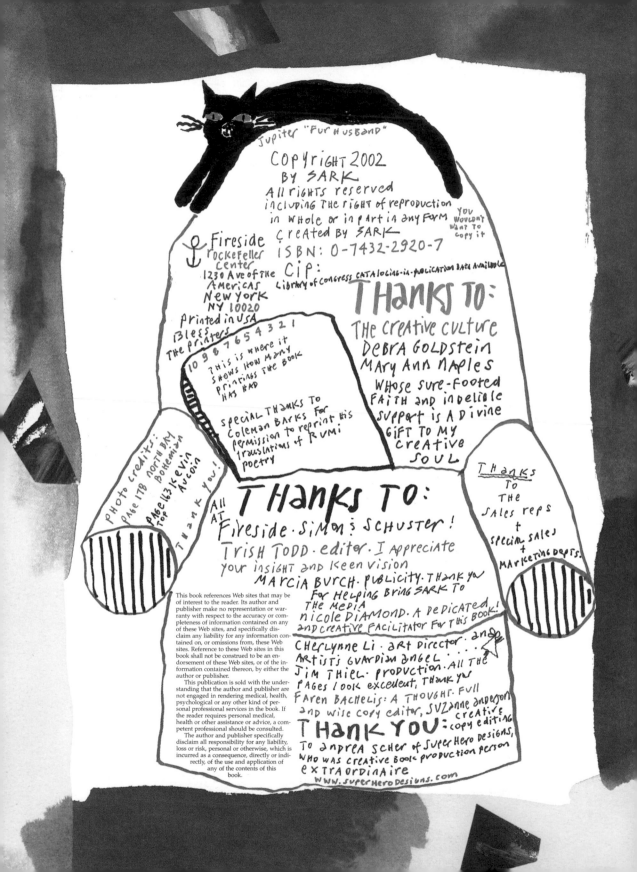

Fireside
rockefeller Center
1230 Ave of THe Americas
New York
NY 10020
Printed in USA
Bless THe Printers

ISBN: 0-7432-2920-7
CiP:
Library of Congress CATALOGing-in-PubLICATION DATA AVAILABLE

10 9 8 7 6 5 4 3 2 1
THis is where it shows How Many Printings THe Book Has HAD

SpeciAL THanks To Coleman Barks for permission to reprint His translations of Rumi poetry

THanks TO:
THe CreATive CuLTure
DeBRA GOLDstein
MARY Ann NAPles
WHose sure-Footed FAiTH and indelible suPPort is A Divine GiFT TO MY CreATive SOUL

THanks To THe SALes reps + special sales + MARKeTing depts.

Photo credits: Page 178 NorTH BAY Bohemian
Page 163 Kevin Aucoin
Thank you!

THanks TO:
All AT Fireside · SiMon & SCHUSTER!
Trish TODD · editor · I Appreciate your insight and Keen vision
MARCiA BURCH · PUBLICity · THank you For HeLPing Bring SARK To THe MeDiA
Nicole DiAMOND · A DeDicATed and creATive FAciLiTATor For THis Book!

CHerLYnne Li · ART Director · and Artist's GuArDiAn Angel . . . .
JiM THieL · production · All THe PAGes look excellent, THank you
FAren BACHeLis: A THOUGHT FULL and wise copy editor, SVZanne anderson creative copy editing

THANK YOU: To andrea SCHer of SuPerHero DesiGns, WHo WAS creative Book production person exTRAOrdinAire
WWW.suPerHeroDesigns.com

THIS BOOK
is
DELICIOUSLY DEDICATED.
TO
MY Beloved BroTHer
andrew JOHN Kennedy
One of MY FAvorite
TEACHers (of SCHOOL and of LiFE)

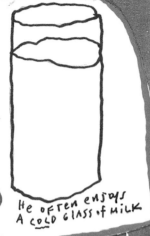

He oFTen ensoys
A COLD GLASS of MILK

VerY Little is needed TO MAKE A HAppy LiFe
Marcus Avrelius

TO:

ScrUMPTiOUSLY. SARK

Pieces of

This is an interactive book, meant to be drawn, written and colored in. Feel free! I made some black + white pages so you could color them

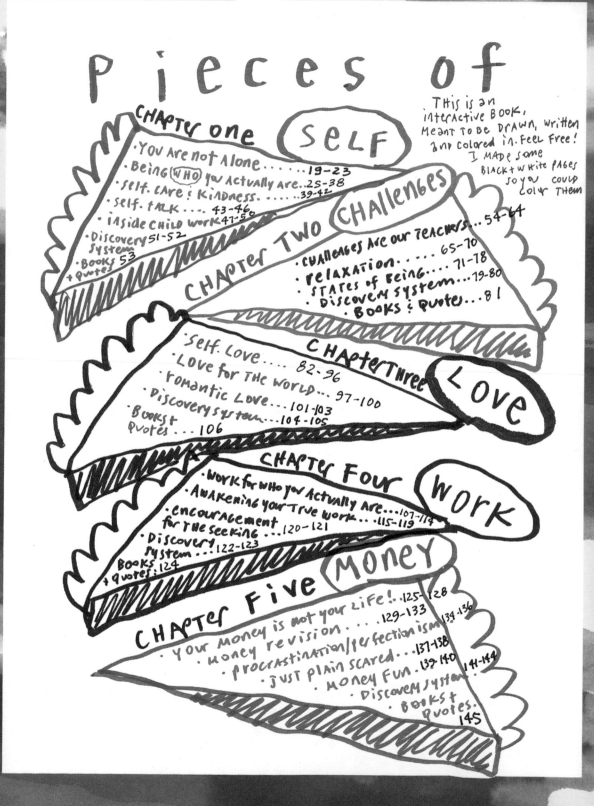

prosperity pie

INTRODUCTION

 **Means:**

Plenty of everything, with enough to share.

I believe that we need to discover (WHO) we truly are, in order to develop inner prosperity.

Exploring time, money, love, work, adventure, inspiration and self, will assist us in asking/answering the following questions:

- ⊚ WHAT contributes to our prosperity?
- ⊚ WHAT lifeskills do we need?
- ⊚ How can we welcome more prosperity into our lives?
- ⊚ How can we share more of our prosperity with others?

I'm also calling this the

 THEORY

everyone deserves a whole pie!

The universe provides for us all every day, no matter how much we have or don't have. We deserve to feel that we are, have and do enough in our lives.

Exactly as we already are. We can infuse our lives with new perspectives on prosperity. By shifting our focus and reawakening our minds and hearts, life will overflow with a profound sense of "enoughness" regardless of what our actual circumstances may be.

We can revel in the luxury of being alive, with full awareness and permission to truly feel that we are (enough) just "as is."

So many of us never, or rarely feel that we are enough. We fill our lives with self-improvement as though we're lacking in some primary way.

We're noT!

Our inner Critics WOULD HAve US
Believe THAT if only we HAD More
_____, or less _____,
or were _____, (THen) we
WOULD FinAlly Be enoUGH.
    YeT wHen we AcTUAlly DO StrATeGize,
MAke CHanGes, THose inner Critics
Become very wily and Use THAT
inforMATion To point ovT How we're still
LACKinG.

        So SneAky

    new Perspectives and TooLs Are
needed. I've Been STUDyinG THese
ConcepTs For MAny yeArs, and still only
GeT GliMpses of FeeLinG THAT I AM
"enoVGH."

        Prosperity prActice
                is
        AssistinG   Me

10

The First Thing I will Admit is
That I'm in A process of Discovery About
Living with prosperity and relaxation.
I Believe Fiercely in Sharing my ongoing
Story of Life, Because it is Your story
too.

Im excited to share what I've Discovered,
and what I still Dont know. I Think I'm
one of the least relaxed people I know.
I Asked my Friend Yofe for Her opinion,
and At First she politely said,
   "OH no, I think you're relaxed."
After I encouraged Her To tell me the
Truth, She Finally said,
   "well, you're the most Fun
   least-relaxed person I know!"

Life often shows us The
contrast of prosperity and relaxation.

Scarcity/Agitation

It is very tempting and often feels necessary to contract ourselves into scarcity and tension/agitation.

The truth is, things fall apart, blow up, get lost, die, become hopelessly tangled, disappear and disappoint.

We are still called upon to find our center, to bake our "prosperity pie" regardless of outside circumstances.

"The paradox is that it's all perfect and it all stinks. A conscious being lives simultaneously with both of those."

Ram Dass

our Lives Are Teaching us

I've chosen to share my life experiences through my writings and drawings, and I write about the "real stuff" as it happens to me.

even when it's unflattering

I am convinced that when we can share our "real stuff," we can then alchemize it into something valuable to bring to the world.

The world will respond well to this way of being, and to the gifts we bring.

We are so full of glorious treasures! Our lives are huge libraries containing gems and sweet mysteries to share with others. Our "ordinary lives" are really a miraculous combination of biology, psychology and radiant energy.

We are so abundantly blessed and I am calling you out to play and be seen (and to bake your own prosperity pie.)

Prosperity pie means expanding
all the good things, and that includes
the pain. For years, I tried to over-
emphasize the light, before I fully
understood that the dark had to be
woven in and worked through first.

We can work with this darkness together.

There are many, many millions
of us on this journey of self-exploration,
and we are kindred spirits speaking
a similar soul-language.

This "language" is one of
Connection, Color, eccentricity,
Humor, Allowing and Compassionate
witnessing.

We can share more of our
turbulence and seeking for
enoughness, with its raw, ragged
edges and places of not-knowing.

We can provide emotional shelter for each other and keen vision.

We can borrow each other's strength and confidence when we stumble and falter.

We can learn to live fully in this very moment.

RIGHT NOW

Where are you? Look around. Whatever you see is a teacher of some kind. Our lives are our Prosperity Pie teachers.

I've written many books and made many mistakes. I've also been sincerely blessed. Much of my earlier life was troubled, and yet whatever wisdom I may have, originated with these experiences.

WHATEVER HAS HAPPENED

TO US

HAS

CONTRIBUTED TO US.

This BOOK of Prosperity Pie Contains:

@ My inventions and Discovery systems for expanding your feelings of prosperity, with examples of old patterns transforming into new ones.

@ identification of obstacles and challenges in daily living, and new ways of being with them.

@ supportive stories and introductions to people living in prosperity and working on all the same stuff you are.

@ Questions for you, designed to awaken your feelings of prosperity, with places to scribble and color your answers.

Feel free to write in the book or NOT. Either way will work.
I have a theory that books Don't even need to be read to be Helpful.
Just Their presence Affects us

There Are Things To Try That Have worked for Me and others, and Many Descriptions of My Mistakes and Failures, which includes places I still get stuck and lost.

WHICH Are plentiful

Mostly, it is an Active Companion to your own journey of prosperity. This Book will serve As A sturdy walking stick, A self. love Magnifier, and A Kind, wise Friend who tells you:

YOU ARE eNOUGH

YOU HAVE eNOUGH

YOU DO eNOUGH

and THEN Brings you Chocolate

We Are All Gifted

Inside of you are Treasures

Here's why:

You can WEAR A TUTU EAT Fruit NAKED
imitate a Sheep CUT your own HAIR
CAVORT in The GRASS Drink lemonade
BAREFOOT Discover inner WEALTH CLIMB
Tall Trees Communicate with angels
Multiply Love EAT DeLicious
FOOD Listen to spiritual Songs
Reinvent How you Are
Receive countless Blessings Deliver Hope
MAKe your creative DreAMS Visible
B R e A T H e
Surprise your Fears TRAVEL
Gently reAwaken Love Forgive
yourself DeSiGN A Brand
new PATH

Inside of You Are TreAsures

You Are not Alone

How Alone Do you Feel?
In your
STUMBLINGS, rAVINGS, cravings,
insanities, obsessions, stubborn
refusals, resistances, complaints?

Do you THINK you're THE
"ONLy one?" Many of us DO. One
of THE reasons I write BOOKS
is To provide evidence THAT we
Are NOT Alone.

THE BOOKS
BECOME
A kind of
SHAReD
JOURNAL
AMONG Kindred
Spirits
i feel THIS AS I'M creATING
someTimes i Feel isolated and scared...

Being able to speak the
          unspeakable
is very power. Full. If we can
Hear another person express where
They Get stuck, or lost, or repeat
A negative pattern
          it BUILDS A Bridge

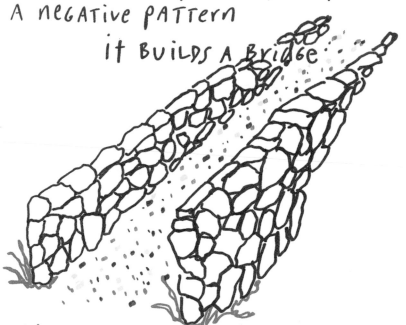

We can use This bridge to Travel
in concert with others As we
Navigate our Lives. It can Feel
very scary To FACE Life when we
Think we Are
          Alone

WE MIGHT WONDER:

WHO WILL CARE FOR US WHEN WE
STUMBLE AND FALTER, BEGIN AGING,
LOSE MOBILITY OR BEGIN UNCONTROLLABLY
DROOLING?

Or AS THE BEATLES SANG,
"WHO WILL LOVE US WHEN WE'RE 64?"

WHO LOVES US NOW??

EVEN WHEN WE ARE SURROUNDED
BY AND WITH LOVE, WE STILL MUST
FACE ourselves ALONE EVERY DAY.

HOW MUCH LOVE GETS inside?

AND

STAYS
THERE?

HOW MUCH is offered THAT is not ABSORBED?

How can we feel love and not
Being Alone

even More Abundantly?
I Believe That we Must
A D M i T

Whatever we Think we're
Alone with, and tell The
Microscopic Truth About our-
selves.

We Are incredibly resilient
creatures if we learn to let it
All Flow Through... if we
Become Transparent

And stop Hiding our Aloneness

We can practice letting More Love in

LOUISE HAY, AUTHOR of
YOU can HEAL your Life and so
many other BOOKS, offers THIS:

A CARD FROM Her WISDOM CARDS WHICH
SAYS:

AT LEAST 3 TIMES A
DAY, I stand WiTH MY
ARMS wide open and SAY,
"I AM willing to leT THe
Love in. It is sAFe TO
leT THe Love in."

You Are not Alone

Borrow FAiTH WHEN you FeeL
THAT You Are

riDe

ALONG

WiTH Me

and

THese

WORDS

Be a lamp, or
a lifeboat,
or a ladder.

Help someone's soul
heal
walk out of your
house like a
shepherd

Rumi

SELF

BEING WHO YOU ACTUALLY ARE

ZOE AGE 5

SAID TO ME,

"OH SUSAN, WHY DON'T YOU JUST BE HOW you <u>ACTUALLY</u> ARE?"

I THOUGHT ABOUT HOW often I'M <u>not</u> HOW I ACTUALLY AM, or MORE IMPORTANT (WHO) I ACTUALLY AM...

I'M often preteNDING, HIDING, in DISGUISE or WEARING A MASK of some KIND.

I'M SO BUSY BEHIND THE SCENES, JUDGING MYSELF, THE SCENERY or THE PERSON I'M WITH, THAT I CONTINUALLY FORGET THE MOMENT I'M ACTUALLY LIVING IN.

WOMAN BALANCING in THE moment

1
2
3

I can offer certain specific descriptions
I HOLD ABOUT "ME." Let's LIST THem:

1. I Don't WEAr UNDerWEAr
2. I'm From MinnesotA
3. I HAte oLives
4. I once CAUGHT A SnAKe WHile FisHinG
5. I Love the Color purple
6. I reAD Books extrAVAGantly

I couLD continue with DetAiLs and
GLimpses Like THese, yeT ALL these
Descriptions Are not "ME." THe
ME is ActuALLy expansive essence
With no BeGinninG or end,
no personA, no AGendA.

    Still, I DweLL Furiously in my
Described personALity, trying to
orcHestrAte and DescriBe THe events
and FeeLinGs of my Life.

I can see THAT we MUST GET BeHiND the DRAMA scene and THE intellectual BABBle, Banter and BlAH·BlAH.

B e H i n D the DrAMA scene

WHen I visit BeHind THe scenes and tovch THe emptiness I Find THere, I run screAMing BACK to my comfort and Control stations.

COMFort STAtion PREDicTABiLity is essentiAL!

control STAtion All CHannels eQUAL

This is All O.K. and part of
The process. Yet My spirit longs for
union with essence, and to surrender
All the BULKy, clunky Business of the
personality and eGo.

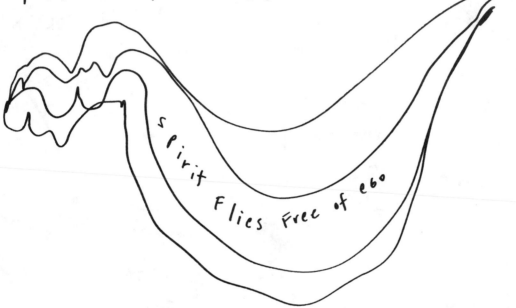

spirit Flies Free of eGo

In order to Feel THAT I AM enouGH
it is necessary To truly Accept and
Live with All of My pArts.
    I cannot turn AWAy From WHAT
Displeases Me, or MAGnify WHAT I FiND
pleAsing ABout Myself.
        i want to Live in THe GorGeous
            neutrAL "Middle"

In order to FeeL THAT (YOU Are enOUGH):
explore your seLF and the WORLD
with consciousness and Compassion.
   Be an emotionAL pioneer WHO tAKes
tender, exqvisite cAre of your very
own souL.
y o u r   s o u L n e e d s y o u r k i n D n e s s
   THe More thAT eACH of us tends
our own souL, the More the WORLD will
prosper.

THis is WHAT we Can
DO For eACH oTHer...
p r o s p e r + s H A r e

   Let's inquire toGeTHer into THe
mysteries.
   I intend to remove More of my
MASKs and veiLs to DO so.

I AM FREQUENTLY AMAZED BY HOW SWIFTLY I CAN ADJUST AND CHANGE. WE ARE INCREDIBLY FRAGILE AND RESILIENT CREATURES!

I AM LEARNING:

- ABOUT CONFRONTING CONFLICT WITHOUT SHAME
- TO PRACTICE SELF-FORGIVENESS MOST DAYS
- TO MAKE MISTAKES AND HEAR ABOUT THEM TRULY (INSTEAD OF DEFENDING, DENYING OR ATTACKING)
- THE VALUE OF EXISTENTIAL VOYAGES
- HOW TO BE UNPOPULAR AND WHY
- TO EXPERIENCE REJECTION IN BRAND-NEW WAYS
- TO TRY NEW THINGS MORE OFTEN (EVEN IF I'M NOT VERY GOOD!)

I AM INSPIRED BY:

- PHOTOGRAPHS OF PEOPLE NOT SMILING   sometimes smiles can be masks
- RAW TRUTH
- INTEGRATED LOVE (WHERE YOU ARE PSYCHOLOGICALLY WHOLE IN LOVE)

Like A perfectly ripe banana

- EARTHY DISCUSSIONS
- RELEASING THE REAL OBSTACLES
- CHANTING
- LIVING LIFE AS AN EXPERIMENT
- PURIFICATION INSTEAD OF PERFORMANCE
- EGO WALLS CRASHING DOWN
- SHARING AND RESOLVING ANXIETY
- SEPARATING FROM PARENTS WITH LOVE
- UNCOMMON QUESTIONS
- VISIBLE HUMILITY

HUMANS ARE VARIEGATED AND REMARKABLE

AS an ADULT WOMan, I AM MoRe
(HUMan) than I ever DReAMed possiBLe,
and in My HUManity I sometimes
see:

Grandiosity   Moments of CRueLty

          evasion and lies   BLocking
enoRMous kindness   receiving

                         eGocentric Motives
SHAme in PHysicAL FrAiLty
          Giving in order to receive

    I AM still an incest survivor. I'm
sometimes A procrAstinAtor, NArcissist,
exAGGerAtor...
     How can this Be?
BecAuse I AM still BLOCKiNG WHO
I Actvally AM
              A HUMan Bean
    I'M not "speciAL." I'M not "the onLy
one."
     I AM not suddenly Going To rid
Myself of WHAT I Judge To Be

"UnDesirABLe QuaLitieS."
My BAsic nAture HAS Been estABLisHed!
 of course, I will continue To
Grow, Be More Conscious, GAin
AwAreness, and there will Be SHiFTs in
perception, revelAtions and new
inroADs...

w H o it nows wHere it will leAd

My intention is To Live More FuLLy
eAcH Moment with (WHO + HOW I
ActuALLy AM) NOT WHO I iMAGine
I will Be one DAY.
 I want to experience More FuLLy
My own enouGH·ness So THAT I
Feel Filled even wHen THings CrumBLe,
or BreAk, or circumstances Seem To
sweep AwAy My "proGress."

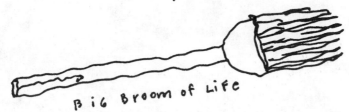

BiG Broom of LiFe

I SAID TO MY MOTHER,

"I've Gotten pretty GOOD WITH plants and aniMALS, WITH TAKING Care of THem. Now I'm working on learning To take care of Me. PerHaps one DAY I'll Be Able to HeLp care for another person."

In My MOTHER's Generation, THey didn't FeeL THey HAD As Many CHoices About TAKING CAre of THemselves First, of BecomiNG (WHO) THey Actually were.

We HAve these cHoices now.

Here I WAS in HiGH SCHOOL, FeeliNG I HAD very Few cHoices:

N
I
C
E

↑ someone wrote THis in My YcArBook...

i Used to iron My HAir so it wouLD Be STrAiGHT and not curLy(:)

34

THEN, AS A YOUNG ADULT, FEELING THAT I HAD
MORE CHOICES, AND WITH VERY little ideA OF
WHAT TO DO WITH THEM.

WHO WE ARE HAS ALMOST NOTHING TO
DO WITH WHAT WE look LIKE, YET THAT'S ONE
OF THE MAIN THINGS THE WORLD SEES.

WHAT DO YOU SEE?

I Believe:

- THAT we can
- Transform "self-help" into "self-explore"
- Spend more time Accepting who we Are
- Make an inquiry into our subpersonalities and responses to our inner critics
- embark on A meditation voyage
- Surround ourselves with Actual teachers and mentors that can support our becoming who we Actually Are
- Actively engage in self-healing/self-exploration work without rigidly defining ourselves by what we discover
- engage more fully into the living of life:

This means Adventure and interactions with other Humans in brand new ways

CHANGE

is

essential

recently, I went THROUGH MY LIVING SPACE and CHanGed All the Furniture and Art Around. All My endearing Arrangements CAMe DOwn or MOved somewHere else. I recycled everythmG I didn't use or Love. AT the close of this process I FeLt new, Free and LiGHTer.

THe objects in our Lives Affect us DAiLy

A CHAiR COULD Be stiff

A VASe Beloved

A HAT infused WiTH Love

SLieer Lost

KinD spoon

Book Blessed BY BATH WATer

"WHO" we Are is often in response To These objects

Of course, All of This can Be CArried "too FAr" (AS I so often DO, BeinG an extreMist)

My friend Larry said,
"Can you just merely inhabit your life
As it is?"

My relentless drive to examine, analyze
and (DO) is most often an attempt to
escape the present moment
and my actual self.

I am learning to reduce the number of
preferences I express. WHAT A relief! All
those preferences are the DOMAIN of the ego,
and it's exhausting trying to get them all met.
I want to see/be brand new all the time.

I want to taste and try things I say
"I HATE." I want to explore places in my.
self THAT feel closed off.

I want to be BRAVE enough to be more
and more ordinary all the time.

CHILDREN are teachers of THIS. They don't care
WHAT we DO AS much as WHO we are

Self·Care and Kindness

We MARCH Around in our Lives DOING our work and CARING for OTHers.

How MVCH DO you truLy cAre for and love your self?

THe Feeling of prosperity BeGins with Ourselves. THe More Full and replenished we Are, THe More we can extend to the world.

We Are Gentle, needy, SOFT, sensitive little Buttons

WHO DeserVe speciAL HandLing

One time, I went to an AirPort WeAring A larGe red sticker THAT SAid FRAGile ON My BACK.

People Demonstrated enormous Kindness
To Me, and reminded Me How little
Kindness I sometimes Give My self.
   As Humans, We need to Give ourselves
Mental, Physical, emotional and spiritual
Care on A Daily Basis.
          exquisite care

Mental Care

NOUrishing THOUGHTS
Mental Discipline
Mental exercise
Mental Fun
Mental cleansing

under
our
Hair
is
our
Brain

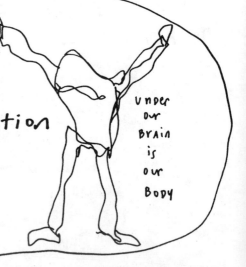

Physical Care

Occupying your Body
Body pleasure
Body repair + restoration
Body rest
Body Movement

under
our
Brain
is
our
Body

emotional care

expressing feelings
identifying feelings
sharing emotions
sitting with feelings
feeling love/loved

inside
it
all
are
our
emotions

spiritual care

communion with nature or spirit
meditation or prayer
surrender to mystery
exploring dimensions other than human

overseeing it all is the spirit

WE ARE SO MUCH MORE THAN
WHAT we can see + feel

Most of us have "inner critics" who
are very active in certain areas. I
have a very fierce health critic (tyrant)
who knows A L L,

Who says things like,
"Why aren't you steaming more kale?"
and,
"If only you had ——————————, you'd
be feeling better now."

I still sometimes view my health as
some kind of test I'm continually failing.

Self-kindness has to step in at
these times and take me gently by
the hand.

We can expand our capacity
and ability for self-kindness.

let
your
two
hands
find each
other
with kindness

Self · Talk

One of the Best Ways to increase our sense of Being (enough) is to change What we tell ourselves.

How do you talk to your self?

Is it kind, supportive and nourishing? Or is it critical, Berating and Diminishing? Most of us hear a harsh inner Dialogue that can be

r e l e n t l e s s

We're often acting from (subpersonalities) (these are conditioned behaviors and strategies for survival developed early in Life) and (inner critics) (These are aspects of ourselves that tell us no, that we're not good enough) as well as (inside children) (each developmental age is represented inside of us, and can "act out" all through our adult lives)

These are all very abbreviated descriptions!

we can
learn
new ways
to
Be

We can learn to identify and work with our subpersonalities, dialogue with our inner critics and give them new jobs, and reparent our inside children.

This gives us access to our adult selves! Then we can apply healthy self-talk on a daily basis and increase our feelings of

e n o u G H n e s s

There are 3 resources I especially recommend for:

inner critic work: embracing your inner critic
and all their books + tapes
HAL and Sidra Stone, PH.D.

subpersonalities: How to get from where you are to where you want to be
and all her books and tapes
Cheri Huber

inner child work: The inner child workbook
Cathryn Taylor

I practice this work daily and am so grateful to have access to my healthy adult self. This adult self needs to hear self-talk that is:

nurturing   supportive   kind   Honoring
acknowledging   Focused   accountable
        strong   Grounded
enthusiastic   Loving   Brave
        nourishing   Thought-full

There Are specific ways to Practice Healthy self. tALK, and I Frequently use writing to CALM and center myself.

Here's A method I use often

1. TAKe your journal, Blank Book or JUST sheets of paper
2. Write Down every worry or Fear, tiny or LArGe, until you Feel empty
3. Do something else, or TAKe A nap
4. sit Down with Those pages and ask your "wise self" to energetically Appear
5. Your "wise self" is your Higher self, spiritual Guide or one-who-knows
6. let your wise self write an answer to each worry or Fear

7. let answers Appear As if you were Advising your Dearest Friend
8. re-read your worries or Fears
9. tear Them up or Burn Them
10. read The new answers and let Them Fill Your Heart

Go and Shine The Light of your self on others

I Know that we All Have A wise self even if we Haven't specifically Accessed it in this way. I Also Know That This self Becomes stronger with use and practice.

When I First started Doing This, it Felt Like I WAS FAKing My wise self answers. It Doesn't MATTer. The method still works.

Here's WHY:
WHen our Minds Are crowded with worries and
Fears, it is nearly impossible To Function in
HEALTHY, positive WAYS.
This in turn Decreases WORRIES *Are An
our Feelings of prosperity.* illusion

PUTTinG our negative self-tALK onto pAper Gets
it out of our HeAds where it can Be seen and
identified. This Also Gives us A chance To
witness our own thought processes, and tAke
A BreAK!

Practicing letting our wise self "answer"
is A power-full WAY to chanGe the energy of
WHAT HAS Been in our HEADS, SWIRLinG and
circLinG in repetitive ways.

So we'll OH, WHATS THE use
bring it AGAIn
it will JUST BREAK
SWIRLinG and circLinG

eventually this Method Becomes A swift
WAY TO chanGe The WAY you Think and HABitually
"TALK" to your self.

HEALTHY self. tALK
increases prosperity

"inside CHILD work"

A simple and power. Full way to experience more inner prosperity is to meet and interact with your "inside CHILDREN." When we are unaware or disconnected from these parts of ourselves, we are missing rich opportunities for personal growth.

When I began this work many years ago, I read all about it, but then couldn't translate the concepts from an intellectual experience to an emotional experience.

With the help of a book by CATHRYN TAYLOR, the inner child WORKBOOK, JOHN BRADSHAW'S work and my COACH and HEALER, PATRICIA HUNTINGTON, I began accessing and communicating with what I call the "inside CHILDREN." suspension of intellect will be help. full as you read on

i found one really MAD scared girl

First, I located and identified what felt like one child, who appeared to me as very thin and screaming. She was about 7, hiding under a piano.

I coaxed her out of hiding, held her and reassured her that she was safe. I worked and played with this child for months before the others began to appear:

The infant
2-year-old
4-year-old
10-year-old
13-year-old
16-year-old
22-year-old

I learned that these kids had essentially been unparented for years, since my adult self had not been actively in charge, and certainly not as an inner parent.

they were all running wild and scared

WHEN I FIRST WORKED WITH THEM AS A GROUP, THEY ALL APPEARED CARRYING WORK TOOLS: A DICTIONARY, PENS, PAPER AND TELEPHONES.

DICTION AERIE

PENTEL

BRIGHT WHITE

A RINGER THAT SOUNDS LIKE A PURRING CAT

I HAD TO PRY THESE THINGS OUT OF THEIR HANDS AND THINK OF "KID ACTIVITIES" FOR THEM TO DO (AGE APPROPRIATE) THEY DO LOVE TO HEAR THE PHONE PURR....

So HERE ARE SOME OF MY INVENTIONS FOR THEM:

THE infant needed A lot of HOLDING AND ROCKING. I WORE A COMFORT CRADLE MADE of CLOTH AND TOOK THE BABY EVERYWHERE WITH ME for AWHILE.

THE 2-YEAR-OLD GOT A tiny HAND-CARVED WOODEN BED WITH A little PAINTED BLUEBIRD on THE HEADBOARD. SHE MOSTLY NAPPED AND SUCKED HER THUMB.

THE 4-YEAR-OLD GOT A FORT WITH lots of toys inside.

THE 7-YEAR-OLD SPENT A lot of TIME WITH ME, HAVING HER HAIR BRUSHED AND ASKING ME QUESTIONS.

inside KIDS love PHYSICAL AFFECTION

THE 10-YEAR-OLD HAD A Best Friend named Missy and spent A lot of Time in nature.

THE 13-YEAR-OLD HELPED with Art projects and loved Going to The library.

THE 16-YEAR-OLD worked with animals and liked Doing Art with younger Kids.

THE 22-YEAR-OLD Moved to BiG Sur, MET Joan BAez and lived with Her and worked As an Assistant, and Began writing A Book.

I Quickly realized that I needed Help with My Kids, so I Hired a nanny named MADeleine. Soon After, Her BOYFriend SAM CAMe From Ireland to Help Her. I Constructed A Tree House WHere they All spent Most of THeir Time.

I've leArned not to tAKe My inside Kids To Many ADult Activities. I've leArned to love THem and Be A MArvelous inner pArent. Here's WHAT THey THink:

WE HAVE the REST MOM in the WORLD!

Discovery System
for
SELF

WHO ARE YOU?

WHAT PARTS of YOUR self DO
YOU HIDE?

WHERE and HOW DO you FEEL MOST LIKE your self?

reminders:

- Be (WHO) you Actually Are
- release self-Judgment
- STUDy your essence
- Become an emotional pioneer
- Develop self-care/self-kindness Abilities
- reAD and study About subpersonalities, inner critics, and inside children
- Activate your HEAlthy ADult self

ADDitional reminders or questions

new views:

- it is safe to take off MASKS + Disguises
- Who you Are is not WHAT you look like, your Age, or WHAT you Do
- you Have new permission To take even more exquisite care of yourself
- THe way you speak To yourself is even more important Than the way you speak To others
- your inside kids Are excited to play with you

Books + resources
SELF

"TAKE CARE to GET WHAT YOU LIKE or you will BE FORCED to LIKE WHAT you GET" George Bernard SHAW

Women of spirit
KATHERINE MARTIN

AWARENESS
anthony De Mello

IN THE SOUL OF RUMi
Coleman Barks

Finding your own NORTH STAR
MARTHA BECK

FeArless LiviNG
RHONDA Britten

StanD up for your Life
Cheryl richardson

www.CAMPSARK.com
www.cherylrichardson.com
www.SABrinAWArdHARRISON.Com

"WHAT is important is NOT WHAT HUrts and pleAses, BUT To see WHAT is TrUe. And THEN THAT TrUTH will operate, not you"
KrisHnAMUrti

CHALLENGES
Are our Teachers

Being (WHO) you actually are is full of Challenges. Challenges help us grow in prosperity and every challenge is a teaching.

What are you learning? Teaching?

Being human means dealing with death, illness, taxes, jealousy, rage, depression, fears, anxiety, loss and change. These are just <u>some</u> of the Challenges.

Here's a recent challenge from my life:

On this particular sleep-deprived day, I was dealing with a legal situation and a visit to the gynecologist, where I was kept waiting in the examination room for 45 minutes in my little paper robe.

Ah, the vulnerability of those miniature paper robes! Your skin even looks more naked under the flourescent lights.

i find it very lonely in there

The Doctor Arrived, and explained that she was "running late" and could only give me a partial exam...

She was Brisk professional and in-a-Hurry i smiled and said it was o.k. inside I was MAD

I then was asked for a urine sample, and after listening intently to the directions, did it incorrectly and dropped the whole thing into the toilet! The receptionist scolded me for not bringing my insurance card, and by the time I left, I was almost crying.

One of the Blessings of this day was my younger brother coming with me to the doctor, and giving me a neck massage in the waiting room.

every waiting room needs a massage Therapist

kind brother

However, my brother's presence also added to my challenges of the day, because I was having difficulty being-who-I-actually-was-in-the-presence-of-another.

i wanted to be cool, strong, knowing big sister

We got back to my house, and I made lunch and tried to fax my insurance card to the doctor.

The fax machine broke the lunch started burning and I opened a box with something I ordered in it AND it was the wrong color!

That's when I tossed a knife across the kitchen. My brother calmly picked it up and wisely said nothing. ⊂━━━━━━

As we ate lunch, I noticed THAT I WAS FLICKING BLACK BEAN SAUCE onto my white comforter!!

After we cleaned it up,
I did it again!

A TRAIL of BLACK BEAN SAUCE

elements and teachings of this day

STATE of being: exhausted
                 sleep deprived
                 hungry
                 scared + anxious

feelings activated: shame, rage, helplessness
                     fear, anxiety, embarrassment
                     feelings of imperfection

The over-riding teaching of this day was
that my resistance actually caused my suffering.
my resistance to <u>being</u> <u>how I actually was</u>
<u>and what was actually happening.</u>

I could have experienced
more self-care if I had:

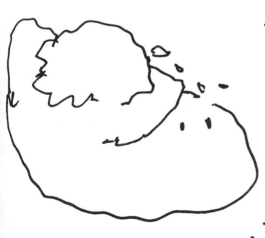

- · changed the appointment
- · nurtured myself as I
   made mistakes at the
   doctor's office
- · not tried to make lunch
- · asked for help
- · asked my brother and
   my self for humor + compassion
   surrendered

and curled up in a little ball
and cried my head off

Many of my challenges spring from:
- Ignoring my body
- Over-riding my body with my mind
- Not occupying my physical body and experiencing a disconnect between mind and body
- Not knowing how to identify what I'm feeling while I'm feeling it

It's all a process of discovery and recovery

Here's another challenge from my life:

On this day, I was reacting and responding to a friend in love. In fact, it seemed that all my close friends had suddenly become couples.

They were
everywhere
it
seemed

every sound and story of "HAPPY couples" FELT LiKE A personal Affront. THey All SAid siMilAr THings:

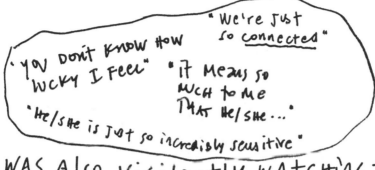

"We're Just so connected"

"you Don't know How Wcky I Feel"

"it MeAns so MuCH to Me THAT He/sHe..."

"He/sHe is Just so increaibly sensitive"

I WAS Also vigilantly WATcHing for signs if neglect and cHange in my Friendstips WiTH My FormerLy single Friends. every Missed Friend-sHip opportunity FeLt LiKe Abandonment

It FeLt LiKe All My self-love work WAS for noTHing. THen, THere is Also WHAT I CAll THe "cult of couples" WHere THe couples want everyone to Be in A relationship LiKe THem.

I LiveD
DAy
After
DAy in THis

CLouD of JeAlousy
and tried so HArd to Get out of it

elements and teachings of this day

STATE of BEING: lonely
ABandoned
Fear of loss
resisting change

Feelings Activated: rejection
Fear of replacement
self-neglect
Hurt

How could I begin to Acknowledge and Accept THAT I Felt hurt and left out, and have THAT Be O.K.?

I knew I WAS Measuring Myself AGAinst THe BACKDrop of My IDEAL self

ideal
self
is
never
lacking

WHo WOULD BE:

· GLAD for My Friends in Love

· Full of reflected Joy

· Filled with utter Happiness for THem

And WHo is THe opposite of iDEAL self?

Mean/BAD Self
WHO WOULD BE:

- Secretly GLAD WHen couples BReAK up
- Full of Bitterness
- Feels left out of everyTHing

Mean
self
is
only
lacking
she needs love too...

I AM neiTHer ideal or Mean/BAD. I'M A perfectly MArvelous Blend of BOTH! My CHAllenGe:

    is To Accept THis

Once I Could(ADMiT) THAT I FelT jealous, Hurt, lefT out, Furious and rejected, I FelT My self. JudGMent lessen.

resisTinG How I WAS Actually FeeLinG HAD Been THe pAin Multiplier.

I TOOK CAre of Myself BY:

- crying
- writing in My jouvnal
- telling A Friend My true feelings

Another challenge in life is something I call "Scarcity Thinking."

Basically, it is guaranteed to stop any growth and keep the thinker in a negative state of being. It also effectively blocks abundance, so that the thought process is rewarded.

It goes like this:

"Oh, there's no point in going there now, I'll never get a parking space."
(Finite number of spaces = Finite number of experiences)

Then you go, and don't find a parking space

"See! I knew there wouldn't be a space!"
(Scarcity conclusion proven)

My friend Roy was experiencing this scarcity thinking and could hardly ever visit me due to his concern about not finding a parking space. I had a party, and hired valet parkers with Roy in mind.

Later, I found out that he was reluctant to come anyway!

WHEN ASKED WHY, ROY CALMLY
responded,
"BUT WHERE ARE THE VALET
PARKERS GOING TO FIND PARKING
SPACES?"
(SCARCITY THINKING SQUARED)

roy's improved
since then...

WHEN I CATCH MYSELF IN THE BOX or TRAP
of SCARCITY THINKING, I APPLY
ACCELERATED FAITH
and
BURST OUT
"Bursting out" often takes THE FORM of
nurturing self. TALK, new perspectives,
reframing and energetic SHIFTING.

· nurturing self. TALK
    Often we are DEALING with
    SCARED "inside kids" and can
    Be Their nurturing "inside parent".
  THE SCARED kids SAY,
"IT's raining! You won't FIND PARKING!
You lost your FAVORITE T. SHIRT! THE
GYM isn't that MUCH FUN and I Don't
Want To Go anyway!"

The nurturing parent responds:
"Let's take the purple umbrella, and I know just where to park, and look! Here's my favorite T-shirt. I'll bet the gym will be fun today."

A bright umbrella always cheers

My favorite T-shirt is a little raggedy

- new perspectives
  Often we just need another way to look at something. A different angle usually works.

- reframing
  This involves restating and reclaiming a natural center.

- energetic shifting
  Sometimes we are caught in a loop of negative energy. Shifting location, clothing, even brushing hair, washing hands will work.

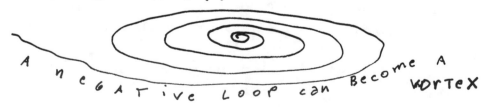
A negative loop can become a vortex

r e l A X A T i o n

We Are MvcH More Likely To experience A sense of plenty when we Are relAxed.

I Feel Like I've Been tyrannized By relAXATion Most of My life, BecAuse it seems THAT I can HArdly ever relAX!

WoMan
All
Wound
up

It's especiAlly pAinFul When people see BeHind MY FAKe "pretending To Be relAxed" DisGuise.

FAKe DisGuises AlwAys FAll off

or if THey sAY,
"JusT relAX!"
How DO you "JusT relax" if you Feel
Tense · TiGHT · AGitAteD?

i wish I could Be More Mellow

65

Sometimes I take on relaxation as an assignment. The interior message is pretty repetitive:

if only you could relax... relax...

My friend Larry was laughing at me the other night because I called him to say,

"if you don't come over by 10pm, we won't have time to play parcheesi and I need to get some sleep, so. when will you be here??"

He calmly replied,

"Susan, are you RUSHING TO RELAX AGAIN?"

and I realized that I was.

rushing to relax

I remember WATCHING OLD Movies where THEY WOULD DRIVE A HErd of Horses into A BOX canyon, WHICH HAD one entrance and no OTHEr exits. I Frequently FEEL This WAY.

AM I the Horses? THE BOX canyon? THE HErDErs? PErHAps I will experiment with This...

THE other DAY, I WAS DOing some Business on THE phone WHEn MY CAT Jupiter suddenly BeGan projectile vomiting,

VOLUMinousLY.

I rushed for paper towels to clean it up, wHile still on the pHone.

As I Bent DOWN, an AGGressive Bee Flew in and started ATTACKING Me. I started "Bee Dancing" to try to escape it. THEn I looked DOWN, and SAW that I HAD WALKED On The CAT VOMit, and now I'd tracked it All over the carpet!

Aggressive Bee

relentless woman

HAPPY CAT

67

I paid attention to how soon I could relax after these events, and it wasn't too long before I was lying in the sun, eating pear slices.

It seems that my relaxation style comes in shorter segments. I think I've been idealizing a certain relaxed type of person, who C A L M L Y moves and speaks. Of course, I imagine that this person is constantly relaxed, or able to relax.

How absurd! I've been so busy judging my ability to relax and deciding that others are (more) relaxed than me... that I've missed my own relaxation!

i want to be present for my own relaxation

Deep
Breath

It's clear to me that the more I can accept my particular style of relaxation, the more I can actually relax!

The truth is, we all get tense, agitated, nervous, tight.

Can we gently turn towards a more relaxed way?

I've discovered that I'm more relaxed than I first thought. I've begun developing a new awareness of relaxation.

i am finding new points of balance

We can relax into our tension.
We can Allow relaxation to Flood in.
We can enter and exit various states of relaxation All the time.
We can Avidly practice new Forms of relaxation.

we can FlOAT in any KinD
OF weATHer

let's expand this ABiLity and tAKe it into our workplaces, schools and cars.

we can leArn To relAx into WHATever it is

STATES of BEING

We Are Here. We Are lost and Found AT the SAme time. THere is surrendering and there Are solutions.

Not Accepting one·self

I Am still surprised WHen I keep Discovering How Little I ActvAlly Accept Myself. As soon As I Feel CertAinTy in one kind or level of self. Acceptance, it Seems thAt another Appears. THis is closely related to lAck of self. love, with A Twist: I think We Ave Being Asked to Accept things we Dont necessArily love. THis is A rich onGoing AreA of inquiry for Me and Many oTHers.

new view:

"Accept everything, judge nothing."
Daily practice of self-acceptance is a
full-time job with plenty of places to
practice. Give yourself gentle guidance
and lots of time.

HABITUAL NEGATIVE THOUGHT

It is easy to get stuck & lost in
negative thinking. There is plenty of
support for it, with expectations of
negativity being more common than
positive thinking.

We can become drawn to other
negative thinkers, and spend our time
repeating the cycle.

negative
energy
can
be
a
frantic magnet

new view:

negative THOUGHTS Are Like non-nourishing FOOD: you can consume it, or offer it, it fills something, but is ultimately empty. you can Gently practice new self-TALK and experiment with a Different Focus.

$\boxed{\text{ADDicted to STruggle, suffering, DrAMA}}$

It is very tempting to engage in All of the ABove. The key word is ADDicted. We can All express any of The ABove states AT various times, but when it feels Like A compulsion, it is very pAinFUL. I FinD that WHen I'M Be HAVing compulsively, I'm usually Trying To FiLL some perceived emptiness.

new view:

If you can identify WHAt need your compulsive BeHAvior is Meeting, you can Choose to Do it Differently. WHen I realize That I Am trying to Fill emptiness, I can Fill Myself in HeALTHier, More nourishing ways.

FiLLinG THROUGH sitting with emptiness

73

rehearsing, predicting, Futurizing

These are all excellent ways to avoid the present moment. I still spend a lot of time in one of these states, or all 3! There is a satisfying sense of control when I'm in the midst of it. Of course, this "control" is an illusion.

new view:

Meditation is perhaps the best antidote for any of the above. Often, I am so busy predicting, rehearsing or futurizing, that I convince myself there's no time left for meditation!

even tiny amounts of meditation will serve you

COMPULSIVE/OBSESSIVE THOUGHT, WORRYING

All of the above are fabulous ways to fill time, drain energy and compromise good health. Often I feel trapped in any of these states by my reaction to outside circumstances.

Once these states are activated,
it is very challenging to get out of it.
I've invested a lot of time here.

New view:

"worry is not preparation"

Cheri Huber

Objective thinking instead of reactive
thinking is very stabilizing. You can
practice this in self-talk.

(repeating addictive behaviors)

I am in and out of an eating disorder
(binge eating) and still need to be careful
with alcohol. These are the substances,
then there are the emotional/mental
addictive processes.

It is very important to remember
the practice aspect here. As Pema Chödrön
says,

"We forget, and we remember, that
is why it's called practice."

I am learning to gently assist myself with the practicing.

New view:

Support is essential. We are so often in shame and alone with addictions. Support can come in a myriad of forms: phone, telepathy, email, group, by mail, spiritually.

OVERWHELM, anxiety

I used to spend a great deal of time feeling overwhelmed and anxious: By time, people, work and any other number of things. I used to begin each day in some variety of one or both of these states. I've learned how to support and comfort myself on a daily basis. Still, I often regress and find myself there again.

remember: regression most often occurs when we are tired, hungry or depleted in some way

new view:

If your inner nurturing parent is engaged and active, it is much less possible to feel overwhelmed or anxious. Also, if you can identify when you are feeling anxious or overwhelmed, and give it room to exist, it will dissolve and trans-form.

widen your field of acceptance

controlling / perfectionist

I'm often trying to "clamp down," "get a handle on it," see what's coming, set the stage, get it right, line it all up, set a policy, make sure THAT doesn't happen again, monitor, pay close attention, do it perfectly...

HOW EXHAUSTING!

New view:

There is no control and perfection is arrogant. Practice Messiness, letting go, and DOING THINGS BADLY.

You can reassign your perfectionist to some other AreA THAT COULD BeneFit From This type of Attention

Fear

I can easily become captivated by Fear. Full Thoughts. These Are contracting States of Being, and usually involve CATASTrophizing in various Forms with Healthy Doses of "WHAT if ? "

new view:

identify A Fear and work with it objectively. recognize the contraction of Fear, and experiment with

e x p a n s i o n of

In opposite state. example:

L o s s v s. p l e n t y

Discovery System
for
CHALLenGes

WHAT Are you CHALLenGes?

How can you experiment with your CHALLenges?

WHo and WHAT Are your support systems?

reminders:

- CHALLENGES Are our teAchers
- WAys of reActing can Be trans.formed
- objective Assessments leAD to new pAtterns
- "ideAl self" is not relevant
- PAin multipliers can Be reduced
- scarcity THiNKiNG Blocks prosperity
- Develop new AwAreness ABout relaxATion
- feeling THAT "you're The only one" is common
- telling microscopic TruTH is HeALiNG
- All of our states of BeiNG can Be identified and worked with

ADDitionAl reminders & questions

new views:

- CHALLENGES Are necessary and support GrowTH
- Blessings live within the chALlenges
- resistance MAGnifies chALleNGes
- relaxATion can Be Defined and redefined To fit who you Actually Are
- Borrow strength and fAiTH from oTHers when you temporarily lose your own
- self.Acceptance is A necessary component to self.love

MAY All your CHALleNGes sweep you cleAn so More love Gets in

Books + resources

Challenges

"He who fears he shall suffer
already suffers what he fears"
Montaigne

anger: Wisdom For Cooling
the Flames   Thich Nhat Hanh

The places That scare you
Pema Chödrön

I can't get over it
Aphrodite Matsakis

The spiritual Dimension
of the enneagram
Sandra Maitri

energy medicine
Donna eden

www.LifeChallenges.org
www.FortheLittleonesinside.com

"If you Don't crack
the shell, you can't
eat the nut"
Persian proverB

L OVe

SeLF. LOVe

THe Deepest sense of Being (ENOUGH)
comes Directly From self. Love.
Prosperity of THe spirit can only Be
experienced From A sturDy platform
of Loving oneself

TRULY   MADLY   DeepLY

THis work is THe most Difficult
I've ever encountered. The capacity
For True self. love is Absolutely
necessary To Love anoTHer, and to
increase self. love experiences, yeT

S e L F . Love is not (TAUGHT.)

self. love is supposed to Be A
Given

YeT WHAT if you were not Given it?

How Do you learn it?

We Are still suspicious of the term "self-love." We Are taught that it is:

SELFISH. SUSPECT. Self-indulgent.
How can we love anything or anyone without

LOVING Ourselves First?

There Are few visible models of HEALTHY self-love. People who Are experiencing it generally don't talk about it, and people who need to learn about it don't know who to talk to about it.

OH DEAR.

I'M
TALKING
ABOUT
SELF-love
not
NARCISSISM

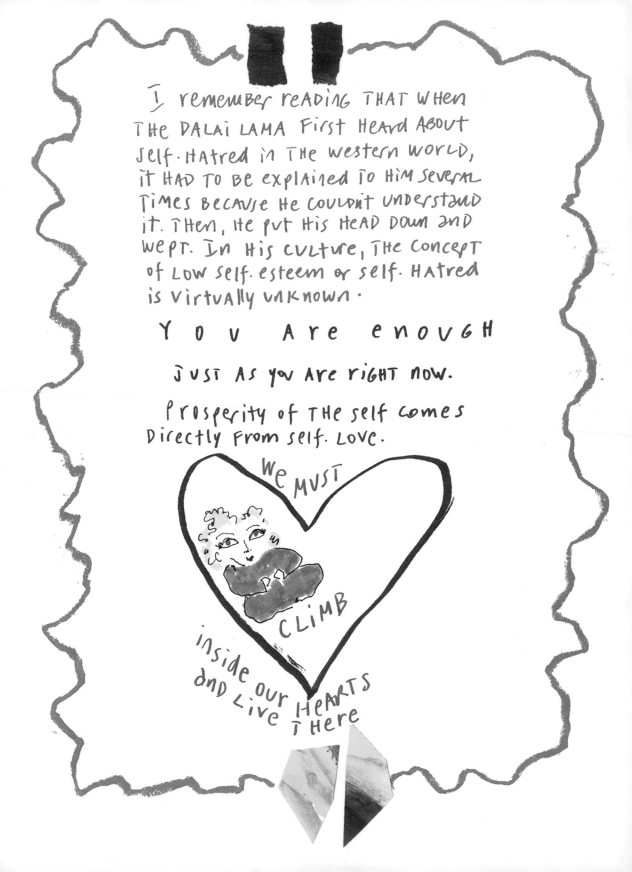

I remember reading that when The DALAi LAMA First Heard about self·Hatred in the western world, it had to be explained to him several times because He couldn't understand it. Then, He put his head down and wept. In his culture, The concept of low self·esteem or self·Hatred is virtually unknown·

Y o u   A r e   e n o u g H

Just as you are right now.

Prosperity of the self comes directly from self·love.

WE MUST

CLiMB

inside our Hearts and Live There

We Are HuSHed in self-love expressions:
Joy-Full MASTurBATion, Going out Alone
with Great pleasure, spending All THe
Money on our own Flowers.

WHAT if someone Asked,
"Are you DATing anyone?"
And you answered,
"I'm reAlly involved loving Myself
right now."

We so often wish To Be rescued,
Distracted, or enveloped inTo THe
"oTHer." we'll DO anyTHing To Avoid
THe BrighT LighTS of reAL self-Love
WHere All of our FLAWS and WeAknesses
Can Be seen and MAGnified.

romantic Love is often MAGnified and Glorified

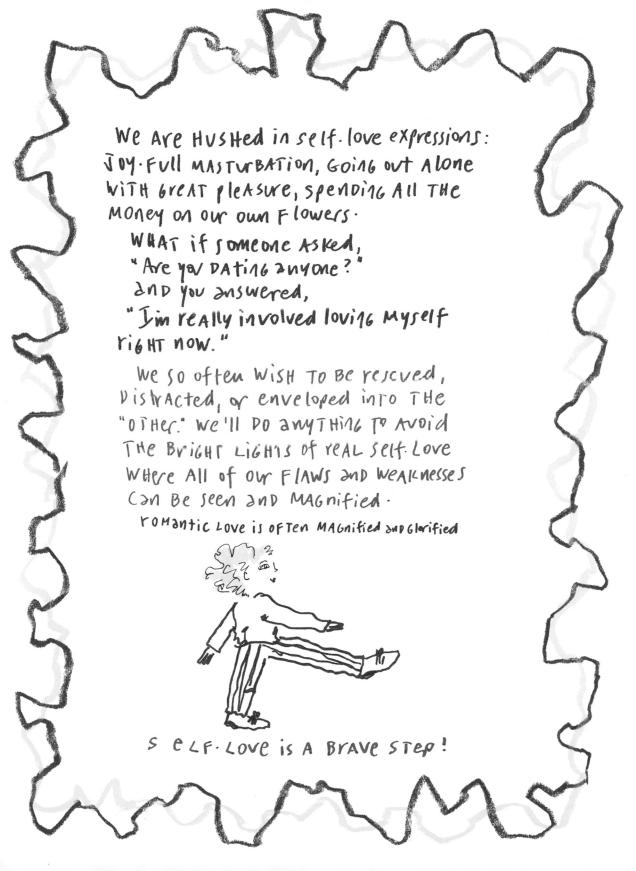

self-Love is A BrAve sTep!

We Are Afraid To stand in THe Glory of self. Love, To celebrate THe

GALA

of our own Being, and revel in THe succulent Love of ourselves.

STAND in THe GLOry of self. Love

LeArning to Love oneself is A necessary and complex ride. We will continue Along in our Lives regardless if How MUCH self. love we leArn to create.

WHere is your self. love locAted ?

My History tells A story About
self. love:
  I WAS loved, nourished, Hugged,
Held, supported By nature, encouraged
By Family, Able To MAKe and Keep
Friends, Given spiritual TeAcHings, sent
To scHool, listened to, TRAVeLed with
and Given Good HEALTH care · · ·
  I WAS Also sexvally Molested, physically
BeAten up and emotionally Misunderstood.
I Then went on To ABuse ALcoHol, TAKe
DRUGS, experience eATING Disorders,
Attempt suicide, HAVe 3 ABortions, no
nourishing work and no place to Live.
  Somewhere in THe weAVing
TOGeTHer of THese 2 portraits WAS
THe choice to experience M ore
or Less Love of seLF.

      "A wounded Deer
       LeAps HiGHest"
         eMily DicKinson

I CHOSE MORE self.love

in THE core WAS A Tiny creature

I BeGan A process of DisManTLing
My "personality" To uncover WHAT FeLT
Like THE TruTH of WHO. I. WAS.
I enGAGed in A long process
of self.examination and HEALing,
WHICH included psychotherapy.
I leArned How To Be

present

for My ACTUAL experience
(not THE one I would prefer to)
Be HAViNG

It took years of practicing being present, and sitting with my "actual experience" to be able to feel

GLIMMERS

of acceptance and to allow my self to be exactly as I am.

During this time, as soon as I could actually identify a feeling or experience, I quickly judged it, named it or figured out a way to get away from it.

It felt excruciatingly painful to (sit with) a feeling I couldn't (control). I would often try to ignore the feelings

but they snuck in past my defenses

89

I began to learn to trust myself and others, to navigate the world, to expand my creativity and to have more experiences of loving my-self.

I also participated in group therapy, (which duplicates your family system in a microcosm and gives you a chance to heal what "was" in your family) in which I learned:

- To accept strong emotions in others and not take responsibility for them
- To hear how my inauthenticity affects others
- To witness fits of rage in others or my-self and know that I am ultimately safe
- To function in family dynamics and social situations in healthier ways.

HEALTHIER WAYS

- TO OBSERVE HOW often I leAve myself To Be with the "OTHer"
- THe extent to which I project feelings
- THAT I Am truly powerful, lovABle and that it is sAfe to Be seen and HeArd

After 12 years of psychotherapy, I Delved Deeper into self. HeAling and self. inquiry By reaDing AUTHors Whose work supported self. HeAling

ORiAH MOUNTAIN DreAmer SABrina wAM HArrison
CHeryl richArDson MAry Oliver
Rumi CHeri Huber
PemA cHODrön
and so many others

I BeGAn working with A HeAler, cHAnged My nutrition And exercise, and explored self. Love more Deeply.

I thought it wAs A One. stop kind of THing. THAT once you could sAy you loved yourself, thAT WAS it.

VOILÀ!

love   All   Around

 I Didn't reALize THe extent of
MAintenance truly loving oneself
TAKes, THe DAiLiness of it.

 My excavations Turned up All
THe WAys I (Didn't) love My. self.

perfectionism   inner
                  critics
      OBsessive THinking
ATTempts to control   Manipulation

new buds were blooming

I began to drop all the inquiry and analysis and get to the self. loving quicker.

In addition to thinking and writing about self. love, I began Living it.

THE angel

in MY Garden
reads a book. the pages
have no words because she is
Living the words

"Living it" feels like this:

A Fiesta!

A Festival of Many Things...

I AM BEGINNING TO:

- TRUST WHAT is offered
- SAY NO CONSCIOUSLY
- SAY yes WHEN I reAlly MeAn it
- Give Myself First WHAT I seek From oTHers
- rest in THe ArMs of the Beloved
- MeditAte willingly
- nourish My self
- run towArds pleAsure
- MAke lots More Alive CHoices
- CHoose AGAin
- let My Bopy leAD THE WAY
- Be ABle To DisenGAGe FroM My Mind
- Live More often in GrAtitude

- experiment creAtively
- sleep and DreAm more AvidLy
- HAve more experiences of BeiNG who I ACtvAlly AM

I now reAlize THAT THe wHole suBject of self·love is just As riddled with DouBTs and DisAppointments and loss of FAiTH As any oTHer love relationship.

Some DAys are so Divine, oTHer DAys Are so messy!

(THere is A comterpoint experience to every item on my LiST)

FOrGiViNG FeBrvARY

self·love cAlenDAr

My love for my self is turbulent and
steady, grounded and insincere, blossoming,
bursting forth and
curling up on the bed crying

I know more of my faults and flaws
now, I'm more familiar with my core and
essence, I am able to practice lovingkindness
and explore more realms of the innercritics.

I periodically go unconscious, fall
asleep and wrestle with self. neglect and
self. hatred. I'm learning to tell my own
truth and trust that I am deeply in
love with (me.)

As I continue to learn and grow, I
express myself through these writings
and drawings. My readers inspire me to
go deeper all the time.

remember when you go deeper
to bring
a flashlight

LOVE for THE WORLD

Our individual prosperity is reflected in the collective prosperity of the world. We are each so capable of such enormous, radiant love.

When tragedy occurs, I am always deeply moved by and aware of the countless numbers of miracles and acts of love that are displayed.

These acts of love eclipse the pain. The pain allows more love to bloom.

One good way to keep love flowing is to make a daily list of what you feel grate-full for.

BLOOM Differently

The world welcomes love and calls for it all the time. We can all take more opportunities to show love.

Here is A Gratitude List From My Journal

I Am Grateful for

Being Able to Share my
voice and Gifts with
The world

Health and Freedom

Perfectly ripe pens

Every person in love,
In my Life

My Vacation to Carmel
and Big sur

9 days off

Choosing to Be conscious

Choosing Again

Andrew living His
teaching dream

My physical space + surroundings

My rather thick arms

My "MOM HAIR"

Attendance to my work

Being invited to be filmed
by PBS

Being asked to have a
radio show

Humility

Jupiter's health and
upcoming holistic appt.

The good movies I
taped

Being Alive
and
Being willing to be dead

WHAT Are YOU GrAte.FUll for ?

romantic love

Oh dear. How do I write about something I feel profoundly unskilled at?

I can certainly share what I don't know, and perhaps some of what I am seeking.

Once I asked my friend Debbie's partner how it felt to be in love with her.

He calmly responded,

"It's a lot easier to tango."

Dances of Love

I marvel at couples who share deep, penetrating intimacy and raging healthy fights.

I shrink with fear at stagnation, repressed anger, passive aggressive acts or cruel silences.

I beam with hope at all of the above, along with loyalty, honesty, microscopic truth-telling, safety and energetic bonding.

I fantasize about truly becoming the person that I long to meet. I dream of a serendipitous union that truly supports my growth.

I have yearnings, longings and desires for romantic love. I'm also bitter, cynical, resistant to even try again.

I'm not sure what I've learned about romantic love except that it's a compelling mystery.

WE ARE DRAWN TO THE MYSTERY

As an experiment, I wrote a personal ad . . .

here's my "personal ad"

offering: one woman.
     writer, poet, explorer, painter.
     eccentric, ordinary, nocturnal, rather voluptuous and very funny.
     psychologically evolved and involved, self-loving.
     sometimes stubborn, grandiose and self-indulgent.
     midwestern, mostly vegetarian, voluminous reader, napper.
     i'm in 4th decade, accepting man in 3rd, 4th, or 5th decade.
     what was your job in kindergarten?

asking: one man.
     humorist, makes things with hands or imagination, cooks.
     self-actualized, emotionally capable and evolved.
     caring, calm, intelligent, humble.
     sometimes neurotic, arrogant or lazy.
     adores children and animals, wide heart, perhaps slightly shaggy.
     self-loving, dreamer, loves his parents.
     shares self and is also self-entertaining.
     kind, splendidly imperfect and a quiet sleeper.
     what blesses you most in your life?

the relationship: unconventional.
     commitment to: joy, pleasure, good health, healthy and active sexuality.
     commitment to: truth and growth in relationship.
     emotionally available and supportive.
     self-love as much or more than love of other.
     ability and willingness to work with own and each other's "stuff."
     honoring and respect of differences.
     shelter and cradling of each other's vulnerabilities.
     belief in mystery.
     open to consider visits with: couples therapist, healer, energy medicine,
     astrologer, homeopath, enneagram advisor, inner critic counselor.
     perspective of relationship as spiritual union.
     i prefer male lesbian, feminist, wise man.

propose:
     email friendship first, then phone, then long nocturnal walk.

Discovery System
for
Love

WHO DO YOU LOVE ?

WHAT WAYS DO you experience self. Love ?

WHere/How DO yN Feer you could grow in Love?

reminders:

- self. love is crucial to loving others
- self. love can be studied and practiced
- sitting with feelings accelerates growth
- gratitude lists help love flow
- romantic love is a privilege and a mystery
- loving is really the whole point

Additional reminders or questions

new views:

- your capacity for self. love is already inside of you
- it is not selfish to expand self. love
- being intelligent isn't necessarily helpful with work of self. love
- the world will welcome your love
- romantic love is learned as much as natural
- it is safe to be partnered or unpartnered

"Love bears all things, believes all things, hopes all things, endures all things" Saint Paul

Books + resources
Love

"It was her completely loving creative being that was the complete source of all living"
Gertrude Stein

The Forgiving self
Robert Karen

No Less Than Greatness
Mary Manin Morrissey

Be The person you want to find
Cheri Huber

Imagine A woman in Love with Herself
Patricia Lynn reilly

Five steps to Forgiveness
everett Worthington

The WAY we PRAY
Maggie Oman Shannon

"It is not the perfect, but the imperfect who have need of love. It is when we are wounded by our own hand, or by the hands of others, that love should come to cure us. else, what use is love at all?"
Oscar Wilde

WORK

WORK for WHO you ACTUALLY ARE

Our society encourages a division between WHO WE ARE and WHAT WE DO. It is an accepted practice to HAVE A JOB you HATE, BARely tolerate, rail against or are bored to DEATH BY.

We FRAGMENT ourselves in order to Arrive AT some "Future Better jos" and STOP seeing THAT THE ONLY time is NOW.

"We can DO NO GREAT THings — ONLY SMALL THings with GREAT Love"

MoTHer TeresA

every jos is an opportunity to sHow GREAT LOVE. I HAD Hundreds of jobs in my 20s, and in every one THere were treasures Hidden in THE weeds.

SomeTimes THe weeds Are THick and TAll...

I knew that I wouldn't stay for very long at any of those jobs, and plotted behind the scenes about how things would be better once I got out...

I now see that I missed a lot of precious moments of NOW while I couldn't be in the present moment.

All of our Prosperity Lies in The Present

no MATTER WHAT it contains!

Our attempts to live for, or in, the future set us up for scarcity. We are continually chasing something we don't yet have.

I eventually dropped out of the "working world" and concentrated on inventing the creative life I had dreamed of. I made so many mistakes. I entered into unconscious relationships and accepted "Help" from people who had mixed motives.

I, HAD Mixed Motives! THere were
So Many CHAlleuges. I Chose not to
(teAcHers)
HAve CHilDreu, eveu THOUGH it WAS A
long-stauDiNG DreAm To Be A MoTHer.

SOMeBODY To CAll Me Mommy

THen, AT 35 yeArs of AGe, I FiNAlly
Wrote aud creAted my FirST Book, THe
Book I'd DreAmed of writiNG All my Life.
I received au ADvauce of $1,200 aud no
Assuraucer thAt auyBODY would Buy it.
I'd Also self-puBLisHed A poster called
"How to Be au Artist," aud HAD HaudMADe
THousauds of these posters to support myself
As I wrote.
THis WAS the work Life of my DreAms
auD niGHTMAres

People DiD Buy my Books aud ART,
aud I kept creATiNG, aud it WASnt THe

BLISS

I HAD IMAGINED.

I WOULD
write, DRAW,
PAint, create

THE WORLD WOULD receive it
and Be Helped in WAys I'd DreAMed of

I WOULD
continue writing,
DrAwing, creating
and painting

I FORGOT A FEW THINGS ALONG THE WAY:

- DOING SOLID PSYCHOLOGICAL WORK ON MYSELF SO I COULD EXPERIENCE AN "INNER PROSPERITY" FROM MY CREATIVE DREAMS
- THAT EVEN TRUE WORK DOESN'T SOLVE EVERYTHING
- THAT MY WORK WOULD NEED SOME SORT OF BUSINESS FOUNDATION, AND WHAT WOULD THAT BE? WHAT ABOUT: FINANCIAL PLANNING, BUSINESS KNOWLEDGE, WORKING WITH A TEAM, BEING AVAILABLE TO ACTUALLY CONDUCT BUSINESS?

I FOUND OUT THAT IN BUSINESS, I WAS SOMETIMES REACTIVE, HIGHLY EMOTIONAL, PRONE TO HIDING OUT, UNAVAILABLE, QUIXOTIC, UNRELIABLE, EGO-DRIVEN, COMPETITIVE AND POSSESSIVE.

I ALSO FOUND OUT THAT IN BUSINESS I COULD BE OBJECTIVE, VERY INTUITIVE, SMART, CAPABLE, INSPIRED, AVAILABLE, PRESENT, HUMBLE, INNOVATIVE AND FOCUSED.

WE ALL HAVE COMBINATIONS OF THESE TRAITS IN OUR WORK AND BUSINESS LIVES. "WORK" BECOMES JUST ANOTHER PRACTICE GROUND.

It serves as the mirror that reflects the things we sometimes would rather not see.

My coach Patricia says, "The majority of working people are coming from an unparented inner 5-year-old. Very few real adults are functioning in the workplace."

THAT DARN MIRROR

I know that business provides many opportunities to learn about and grow from:

· reactive, fear-based thinking
· scarcity mentality
· crisis planning
· procrastination/perfectionism

So many people imagine that if they

JUST DIDN'T HAVE TO WORK

everything would be perfect, or at least M U C H B e t t e r.

AHA! They're forgetting about their (MINDS) and what happens when we're alone or feel purposeless.

For a while not working goes swimmingly.

SWIMMINGLY

eventually boredom and restlessness and a fair amount of discomfort set in, or as my coach Patricia says, a "DIVINE AGITATION" and this is good.

We can then see clearly and begin
to decide what our soul's true work is.
You can also make this same inquiry while still
working at something that may not be your true work

relief is not found in not working.
True relief is found in surrendering
into the work — whatever it is.

I am aware of the utter luxury
and responsibility we have in our
culture to even ponder these things.
There is work that is not negotiable:

In order to eat, be housed, have
medical care.

Still, we must function within the
systems we find ourselves in, and
then assist in designing and building
new systems to share with others.

WHO Are You?

WHAT is Your real work?

A Wakening your True Work

I Applied A collage technique To discover/uncover my true work. Here's one From my 1993 Journal:

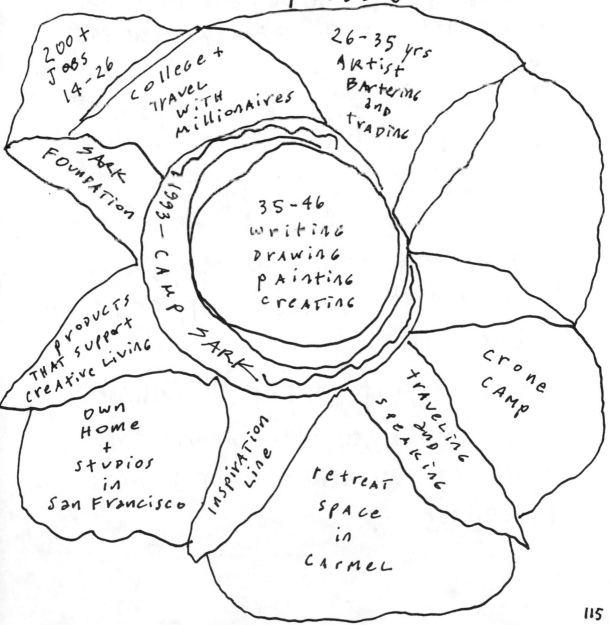

200+ JOBS 14-26

COLLEGE + TRAVEL WITH Millionaires

26-35 yrs Artist Bartering and Trading

SARK FOUNDATION

1993—CAMP SARK

35-46 writing drawing painting creating

PRODUCTS THAT SUPPORT creative living

Crone CAMP

OWN HOME + STUDIOS in San Francisco

INSPIRATION Line

TRAVELING and SPEAKING

retreat space in CARMEL

EVERYTHING we've Done Contributes
and Gives Clues to our True work.
All My rejections and Misguided
Attempts to publish and share my work
Are part of the collage, and in FACT,
support the GROWTH I AM experiencing
now.

NOTHING IS LOST OR WASTED

NO MATTer How MUCH we MAY judge
it, or HATE it, or Accuse it, or refuse
To Honor it.

It's All just part of the collage.

I Like to say, when people Ask
About my education, THAT I went
to collage...

All of my jobs (or most of them) added something to me that was necessary.

Archery instructor, factory worker, waitress, sign painter, baby-sitter, art teacher, office worker, salesperson, stocker, packer, driver, cook, caregiver, organizer, housecleaner and hundreds more. Each contributed something unique

In order to awaken to our true work, we need to wake up from whatever trance we're in, and plan to shift or change as necessary.

The author Barbara Sher says, "keep your day job and tell the truth about the rest of your time."

read: <u>I could do anything: If only I knew what it was</u>
by Barbara Sher

How Do you actually Find that truth?

Many people work at jobs that Drain or frustrate them, and then feel THAT there is literally no energy left to plan for their (True work.)

This is an illusion

If you hold your (True work) as your Highest purpose, you can then take other work that supports that.

MIGHT Be jobs that require little to no "Thinking"

Sometimes, True work Develops out of doing other types of work.

Stay alert for what feels Like your True work.   it will glow

True work will Multiply as it is Discovered. you can Be willing to awaken and activate your True work at any time.

Let your True work
GLOW

SOME THINGS TO TRY:

- DO A COLLAGE of your work and life AS it is now. THEN DO A COLLAGE of WHAT you WOULD LIKE it to BE. THIS Comparison is ACTUALLY A Manifesting Technique

READ <u>CREATIVE VISUALIZATION</u> BY SHAKTI GAWAIN

- I AM your interviewer, and I AM ASKING you, "WHAT is your true work?" WHAT is your answer?

- WHAT can you DO with The energy and Time you spend complaining or criticizing your present work? if you DO complain or criticize...

- Write Down one MicroMovement (tiny step) That you will DO to locate or expand your True work. Write Down A completion Date and reschedule AS necessary. *5 minutes or less in length*

- ASK A Close Friend to Describe in writing WHAT your true work is, AS your friend sees it, and MAIL it to you.

- WHAT WOULD it FEEL Like if you COULD SAY, "I've Found My true work and I'm utterly HAPPY!"

<u>N</u>OT in an IDEAL WAY, BUT in A real WAY!

en(COURAGE)ment for The Seeking

WHAT if you're out of work and
HAVen't yet Found A JOB?

it's scary

The space Between [no work] and
[work] can Be immense and seemingly
impossible.

no work   It (is) impossible   work
in Those moments.
See if you can stay
present with yourself
During such A Time.
Feelings such As shame,
Despair, Hopelessness, Terror,
rAGe, Helplessness, worry and
anxiety MAY surface.
LeT Them surface.
Those Feelings Are Actually propelling
you into new ways if Feeling and Being.

it's True.

One DAY you will
FinD yourself HEADED
To work.

You will BArely
remember WHAT it WAS LiKe
With no worK. Yet All oF THose
SAMe FeeLiNgs Are inside of you.
leT THem surFAce even wHen you've FounD worK
    Our (reAction) to HAviNG worK or not
HAviNG worK is THe MOST CHALLeNGiNG PArT,
anD our (resistance) To FeeLiNG WHAT we FeeL
ABout it CAuses THe GreATesT pAin.
    If you're seekiNG worK, Dont Do it
Alone! THere Are MessAGe BoArds, pHone lines,
BooKs, people WHo would eAGerLy turn towAvd
you to HeLp.
    W orK ALwAys surFAces.
    I send you tAll CourAGe, Deep FAiTH,
anD *UnSHAKAB1e certAinTy.

* B orrow mine if you're temperArily low

121

Discovery System
for
Work

WHAT is your work?

Do you love it?

WHY/WHY not?

WHAT is your True work?

How can you
plan for This?

reminders:

- Division Between WHO we Are and WHAT we Do is encouraGeD By society
- every JOB is an opportunity To sHow GreAt love
- "work" is A Mirror for THe rest of your Life
- not workinG isn't THe answer
- CollaGes Are Useful to AWAKen True work
- noTHinG we Do in work is lost or WAsteD
- you can preserve your true work WHile Doing oTHer work

(ADDitional reminders or questions

new views:

- you Are not your work
- your work Life will provide clves and answers About your True work
- THere is room for everyone To Be Doing His or Her True work
- work is your perfect TeAcHer
- every type of work HAs CHAllenGes
- Divine AGitAtion is A GooD THinG
- you can receive support for your work

MAY you work priMArily with your HeArt   123

Books + resources
WORK

"insist on yourself
never imitate."
Ralph Waldo Emerson

Orbiting The Giant Hairball
Gordon MacKenzie

Self-promotion for The Creative person
Lee Silber

The Lost Soul Companion
Susan M. Brackney

Finding your Passion
Cheryl Richardson

The e MYTH revisited
Michael Gerber

Take Time for your Life
Cheryl Richardson

www.campsark.com (lounge + chat message board)
www.howmuchjoy.com

"The aim of life is to live
and to live is to be aware...
joyously, drunkenly, serenely,
divinely aware."
Henry Miller

MONEY

Your money is not your life!
it just feels that way sometimes

Dealing with money in our lives can feel terrifying. There is a great conspiracy of silence and shame with regard to money.

Writing about money feels as intimate as writing about sexuality.

My experiences of writing about intimate matters has been resoundingly positive and healing. I'm a recovering procrastinator/perfectionist who is/has been in hiding about many money issues.

if money was on the table
I was under it

Whenever we can shine a light on what scares us, it illuminates the scary parts and enables us to see/heal them.

We are all involved in the same money system, yet we don't share our experiences openly or very often. We lie awake at 3 a.m. worrying about bills and have money triumphs alone.

HOW ABOUT THOSE BILLS? (OR BOO?)

WHAT if I Haven't planned Adequately for Health Care, retirement, College, Charities...

We are taught not to tell about, share or show the money in our lives. Open dialogues about money are as rare as a well-balanced checkbook or no credit card debt.

We DREAM ABOUT our IDEAL money
Selves and LIVE in terror of scarcity
or LACK. We WATCH The T.V. news and
READ PAPERS for signs and evidence of
Decline, Collapse, and DOOM.

A HEAD

iDEAL
Money
Self
WOULD

STride confidently AHEAD

We clutch, Grasp, HoArd or spend
Wildly and unconsciousLy. We MEAsure,
Compare, Feer Jealous and Judge.

We Avoid leArning new money lessons
and HAve Few or no support systems for
our money Miracles or MisTAkes.

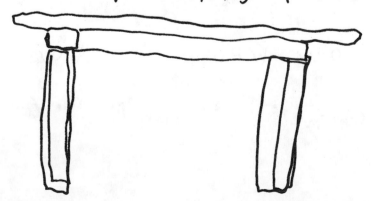

STURDY
PLATforms
of
support

We All SAY we want MOre money
and then DoN't consciously practice
WHAT DRAWS it to us.

we DRAW it
To ourselves

We lie About our money and invent
Stories ABout WHAT we're DoiNG with
it.

We MAGnify

MONeY

and MAKe Our WHOle LiVes ABout it

we Are MVCH more THan our money

Money re·vision

All of our Habits and Beliefs About Money Are leArned. We can leArn new ones.

We Are in A Time of AcceleRAted GrowTH and CHANGE in so MANY AreAs, especiAlly money.

SomeTiMes GrowTH looks Like crisis

WHY would your previous WAys serve you?

We're All so scAred of lAck and Decline, Yet turn AwAY From leArning new systems and METHODs To CHANGE THAT.

WHY?

BecAuse we're AFrAid they won't work!

We GrAsp TiGHTLY onto our previous Systems, BArely BreATHing.

new vision is needed

Time for new GlAsses THAT see Money in new wAYs

We can:

START A MONEY JOURNAL

Many of us only deal with money in our heads or checkbooks. A money journal can be a repository for fears, dreams, hopes and new ideas.

Here's some pages from my money journal:

July 16. 1999
San Francisco

I intend to live fully, prosperously and consciously with regard to money in my personal ; professional Lives

with compassion for my self

When I think of Money

I hear words like: Freedom, security, scarcity, extravagance, indulgence, terror, denial, rage, power, mystery and tedious

✷ I want to identify money areas that are stuck, parched, unexplored, rigid and unclear.

AT THIS TIME, I think these areas are:
· Financial strategy and projections
· Bill paying and record keeping
· expanded investments
· Consistent savings & planning for savings
· Tithing
· Trust funds and tax planning
· setting intentions and goals

✷ I want to identify money areas that are juicy, alive, supportive, unusual, creative and nourishing.

AT THIS TIME, I think these areas are:
· My home ownership and mortgage payment system
· owning my car
· Doing this prosperity journal

- CHECKBOOK SAVINGS METHOD
- MONEY JARS
- BUYING BOOKS and ART SUPPLIES
- SOUL BLESSING TRAVEL and ACCOMMODATIONS
- SETTING UP PERSONAL FINANCE CATEGORIES and NUMBERS
- SEEING THE NEED FOR NEW ASSISTANCE
- THE INVESTMENTS I HAVE SET UP and PAID INTO

Books Are an excellent investment

COMMON MONEY FEAR VOICES and INNER CRITICS

- OH YOU'LL NEVER STAY WITH IT, YOU ALWAYS QUIT
- YOU'LL BE LONELY IF YOU HAVE TOO MUCH MONEY
- LET SOMEONE ELSE DO IT
- HANDLE ALL THAT LATER
- WHO CARES, WE JUST DIE ANYWAY
- YOU HAVE ENOUGH AS IT IS
- DON'T BOTHER ME
- I CAN'T BE EXPECTED TO LEARN and MANAGE ALL THIS
- OTHER PEOPLE ARE JUST BETTER AT IT
- WHAT IF YOU FIND OUT YOU HAVE LESS THAN YOU THOUGHT?

YOU ARE NOT ALONE
WE ALL HEAR THESE MESSAGES

START A (Gentle) Money support system

This can Be A "Group" (just you and one other!) using whatever money book speaks most deeply to you as a guide. Have conversations about money with friends and say what's scaring you or surprising you.

My friend eLissa and I share "money miracles" with each other, from repayment of debts, to discovered dollars in a checking account.

MONEY is NOT THe problem!

We rush to make it into one so we can justify our fear. revise now how you act, speak and think about money.

remember to be objective instead of reactive about money

I'll be doing all the same work too.

WALK THROUGH A new Door

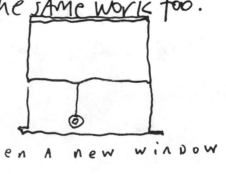

open a new window

Procrastination/Perfectionism with regard to money

Do you consistently put off dealing with your finances? Most of us do. It honestly <u>never</u> seems like the right time.

Do you recognize yourself in any of these phrases?

- Maybe it will just go away/get better
- I'll look at it later
- it can't be that much/bad
- I'll handle it when I have to

Procrastination gives us a marvelous gift:

(More Time)

We all imagine that others are really organized and together with their money.

MOST people are N O T.

Honor and welcome your procrastination,
it serves you.
   If you wish to have a different response
than procrastination, you can change that
habit and behavior when you're ready, or
not!
   Perfectionism
   Do you recognize yourself in any
of these phrases?

· it's too late to invest now
· When I find the perfect ————,
   then I'll ————
· I need to be a lot more knowledgable
   to even attempt that
· That's just not how it's done!

   As a precious perfectionist who
is still actively practicing, I can
tell you that it gives something valuable
to me:

   NOT BEING WRONG

If I never venture outside of my money comfort zones, then I'll never be wrong! i still love to be right (or think i am)

I'm gently looking at new ways to experience this, so I am not repeating the same restriction over and over again.

Money is another marvelous mirror that can reflect where we're hiding.

WHere
Are
You
Hiding?

JUST plAin SCAReD
ABout Money

WHAT Do you DO WHen you HAve little or no income?

Be SCAReD.

Sit THere For A wHile, 2nd then Activate your creativity 2nd

create some Money.

Money c2n Be invented With A Different Attitude 2nd SHiFT in perspective.

It is very tempting WHen you HAve little or no Money, to think THAT someone HAs it, 2nd you HAve to work for Him or Her to Get it.

WHile it MAy Be true in A reAListic Sense, or From one point of view,

WHAT ABout your unexplored GiFTs?

Treasures

o pen up your GiFTs

HAVE you truLy invested Time and energy in offering yourself to the world, in service, in exchange for money?

and not in the usual ways only.

I HAVE Been Homeless, on welfare, Lived on less than A shoestring, in DEBT

eventually, I was ready To start A new money chapter.

SCArcity is very compelling (scare city).

You can Move out of This city!

I Acknowledge the pain and FEAr you may Be feeling.

MOVE OUT of SCAre CITY

please turn towards new forms of work and Assistance

Money Fun

I can just hear you exclaim,
"Fun? What fun?"

We know that money can buy fun things, we just dont realize that money itself can be fun.

There is a wonderfull game by the author of <u>rich Dad, Poor Dad</u> called the Cash Flow game. Just reading about it is inspiring. I've been too shy to play it yet. Perhaps soon!

We can spend our money consciously and with joy.

We can save with integrity.

We can share our "Money Miracles" and set up rewards for ourselves.

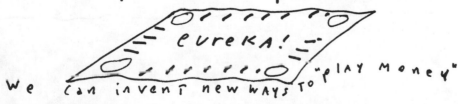

We can invent new ways to "play money"

We can invest in ourselves and trust in our creative money abilities to create more JOY.Fully.

Money can rAzzle-DAzzle,
BuilD Bridges, Buy MILK, sAve children
it will Follow your leAD

Money flows toward GOODness, and THe More Fun we can HAve, THe More it will AppeAr.

We can HAve Fun SHAring Money with OTHers in innovAtive ways.

Promote Money Fun!

Discovery System for Money

WHAT ARE YOUR EARLIEST MONEY MEMORIES?

WHAT WERE YOUR PARENTS' OR CAREGIVERS' MONEY STYLES?

WHAT WERE YOUR FAMILY'S MONEY BELIEFS?

WHAT Are your current Money Beliefs?

BiGGEST Money FeAr?

BiGGEST Money DreAM?

WHO supports you in prosperity?

WHO DOESN'T support you?

How can you re·vision your experience of Money?

reMinDers:

- Your money is not your Life
- noBoDy is iDeAL with Money
- open DiALogues ABout money Are rAre
- All of our Money HABits and Beliefs Are leArned
- creAte A Money JournAL or Group
- Gently Form Money support systems
- ProcRAstinAtion is A GiFT
- Perfectionism is A sHelter
- Money is A MArvelous Mirror
- if you're scAreD, sit THere, THen creAte some Money
- Money itself can Be Fun
- As you reAD + THink ABout Money, BreATHe

(ADDitionAL reminders or Questions)

New Views:

- you Are sAFe
- HumAns cAn cHAnGe HABits very Quickly
- MAke More Money "mistAkes"
- Trust in your own process with Money
- Your Money style HAs virtues
- Money is Just one MeAsurement
- retire THe MeAsurer
- Money is A GiFT to you and The worLD

PrActice Money-nourisHing THouGHts and Beliefs

Books + resources
Money

"your pain is the breaking of the shell that encloses your understanding" KAHLIL GIBRAN

Seven Laws of Money
MICHAEL PHILLIPS

Sex and Money Are Dirty Arent they?
CHERI HUBER

RICH DAD, POOR DAD
ROBERT T. KIYOSAKI
with SHARON L. LECHTER CPA.

Money SHY to Money Sure
OLIVIA Mellan and Sherry Christie

Creating Money
SANAYA Roman and Duane Packer

everyday I pray
Iyanla Vanzant

WWW.RICHDADPOORDAD.COM (CASH FLOW GAME)

Chaos
Aside,
Future
Is Great

Time

Fresh Perspectives

Time prosperity

It is very tempting to frequently think that there isn't enough time. This is time scarcity. New perspectives are needed.

WHAT TIME WOULD you think it WAS if there were no clocks?

rest in Timelessness

IF Time wasn't A FACTOR, WHAT WOULD you DO/not DO?

see Time AS A choice

How Do you keep Time, or Does it keep you?

Keep Time Fluid

We can Trust Time to keep itself. We can meet Time Along the way and view it As A collaboration instead of an Assignment.

Time is A supreme GIFT

Time shrinks and expands
According to our mood..

BIG
TIME

Tiny Time

Time is an illusion.
Time can Be viewed As an enemy
or A friend - it Doesnt care.

Time will Definitely Tell
on you.

Y e s
s He
WATCHED
A
L o t
BUT
n e v e r
reAlly
HAD   T i m e

Altering your sense of Time

I am usually experimenting with time in various ways, and here's what I've discovered:

If you're feeling crushed, pressured, squeezed or pinched for time, you can call in the

Time Stretcher

The Time stretcher is benevolent, very advanced and capable of actually moving time by altering your perception of it.

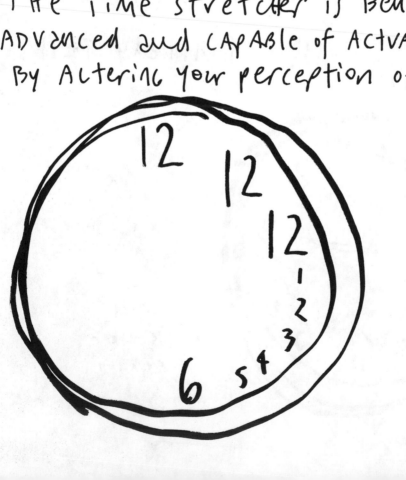

YOU MIGHT SAY,
"I'll never Get This Done in 8 Hours!"
THE TIME stretcher HAS THE ABILITY TO CHANGE THE CLOCK. Suddenly, 2 extra Hours Appear. If you've called in THE Time stretcher, you MIGHT HEAR yourself SAY,
"I'M Getting So MUCH Done, and it isn't even close To the cutoff!"

MiRacles of TIME

You Can PRACTICE CALLING in THE Time stretcher By experimenting During periods of Time pressure. It seems THAT JUST BEING open To the TIME stretcher ACTIVATES it.

Of course, sometimes it Doesn't Work. Usually When it seems THAT it's not working, I HAVEN'T Given it enough TIME!

I HAVe repeAted success with The
Time stretcher, and invite you to
experiment with it.

WHAT ABout WHen you're Feeling
Tortured, Bored, restless or AGitated,
or you're WAiting in an endless line?

You can call in THe

Time sHrinker

THis Quick Technique can Help
You compress A slab of Time into A little Bit.

You MIGHT SAY,

"THis line is so long and Moving so slowly!

Suddenly, you're tAlking to A GArdener
From englaud WHo sHares the contents of
Her Travel JournAl with you...

if
you look
inside
THis
BAG of
Treasures...

You look up to see that an hour has turned into 10 minutes.

Both the time shrinker and the time stretcher are standing by to be of service.

In India, there is a concept that the timing of a thing is more important than the thing itself. If you do something at a prescribed time, you will not be successful if the energy isn't right. If you set off on a trip at the wrong time, or with the wrong energy, certain things may occur that wouldn't have had you waited.

YOU COULD BECOME QUITE ALTERED ON AN ELEPHANT

I usually create what I call an "elastic schedule" that can bend and stretch to allow for energetic shifts.

"it's all just energy"

PATRICIA HUNTINGTON

This concept requires tuning in closely with energy. Not just your own, but that of the world.

Children naturally do this by delaying in all sorts of ways. The "delays" are often a way of sensing and responding to energy.

You can practice all sorts of methods to alter your sense of time and create more abundant time experiences.

It's a fascinating way to experience Life.

Discovery System
for
Time

HOW DOES TIME ACT IN your life?

WHY?

WHERE DO you need MORE TIME?

HOW?

MAKE NOTES ABOUT USING TIME Differently

DOING WHAT?

reminders:

- How you use time is a choice
- keep time fluid
- experiment with the time stretcher, and the time shrinker
- study intuitive time concepts
- give yourself fresh perspectives
- time can be a collaborator, not a taskmaster

Additional reminders or questions

new views:

- time can be viewed apart from clocks
- time is variable, not fixed
- elastic schedules can be productive
- timing is as, or more, important than whatever the activity is
- time will alter according to what you bring to it
- time is your own invention

May you develop an exquisite, uncommon relationship with time

Books + resources
Time

"Until you value yourself, you won't value your time. Until you value your time, you will not do anything with it."
                    M. Scott Peck

Inner Peace for <u>Busy People</u>
          Joan Borysenko, Ph.D.

<u>Time and Again</u> Jack Finney

<u>Living your Best Life</u>
          Laura Berman Fortgang

<u>Conscious Living</u>
          Gay Hendricks

The Blessings <u>Already Are</u>
          John Morton

<u>Cultivating Delight</u>
          Diane Ackerman

www.wildmind.org
www.iyanlatv.com

" Adopt the pace
   of Nature. Her secret
      is Patience."

         Ralph Waldo Emerson

inspiration

(WHAT) inspires us?

We are filled up by inspiration.
I'm inspired by unusual invitations.
My friend Leigh had what she called
"show + tell" at her home. We were
asked to bring a story or object to share
with the group.
There were 15-20 women each with a fascinating story

There were songs, books and clothing
being shown and shared. Poetry was
read, tears shed, laughter abounded. I felt
illuminated.

Sometimes inspiration appears suddenly:
I laid on a beach at night, by moonlight,
The sand still warm. A flock of geese flew
over, and as they got low and close, I could
hear a scritchy sort of concentrated hiss of
all of their wings flapping simultaneously.

I shuddered with delight and felt
my soul carried with the sound.

inspiration comes in many forms:

On this day, I walked up a steep hill to my house and got very tired, so I flung my backpack down on the sidewalk, and laid down using it as a pillow. The next thing I heard was a man's voice,

"You cant lie there!"

I. didn't open my eyes, and replied with a smile,

"Who says?"

I then opened my eyes to see a very well-dressed, very drunk man, weaving slightly, holding a brown paper bag. He said,

"You're a rebel arent you?"

I said that I was, and always had been.

"Well, after today, you dont need to worry anymore."

I asked him why, and he just smiled knowingly, and said,

"Also, you've forgotten that

you're A BeAUTiFUL womAN! AND
FUrThermore, you HAve A GreAT cHiN
AND iF I WAS youNGer, I WOULD Try to kiss it!"

    AND He WALKed oFF. I LAID THere iN
THe SUN FeeLiNG BLessed, AND ThiNKiNG THAT
we never KNow How THe ANGeLS miGHT Be
Dressed. i THiNK THAT He WAS AN ANGeL DisGUiSed AS A DrUNK Person

    Inspiration loves us to visit:

    My Friend YOFe iNvited me to come
WiTH Her wHiLe SHe swAm iN THe SAN FrANcisco
BAy. I SAiD I'd love To WATCH Her From THe
BeAcH. I LAID oN THe SANd GriNNiNG AT Her
iN Her Little BATHiNG cAp, oUT AmoNG THe
wAves.

Her SAUCy STrAw HAT

    I BeGAN WATCHiNG A womAN weAriNG
A STrAw HAT FLoATiNG NoT FAr From
SHore, ANd kNew we wOULD meeT.
WHeN sHe Got oUt oF THe WATer, I
Greeted Her, ANd THis is WHAT SHe SAid:
    "Most people DoN'T kNow How to reLAX.
I tell THem iF you Just Get iNto THe
oceAN, it wiLL Do it For you. you DoN't Need
to Do ANyTHiNG else."

158

Sometimes inspiration can
feel scary:
While staying at a resort in Arizona,
I went for a walk at dusk in the desert.
Out of the bushes came about 10
prehistoric-looking creatures, kind of
like boars, but somehow oddly like
rabbits. They all had apples in their
mouths and babies trailing behind.

I stood and took some deep breaths,
and sensed their energy, which seemed
sweetly purposeful. I felt I had wandered
into an alien landscape! Later I found
out that they are a species unto themselves
and are called javelinas, and eat dates
that drop from the trees. They can be
vicious if cornered (so am I) but can only
see about 4 feet in front of them (I'm also
nearsighted).
        Maybe I am related

inspiration is Born of suffering:

Having once again just gotten the news that my mother was hospitalized and in intensive care, I looked out my window to see a ladybug trapped in a spiderweb. Feeling uncommonly sad and helpless right then, I couldn't stand to watch the ladybug be consumed. I looked more closely to see that it was an abandoned web, so I rescued the ladybug and brought it inside.

I got a pin and a magnifying glass, and spent about an hour disentangling the web, which was wrapped tightly around the ladybug. We began communicating telepathically so that when I would hold down one strand of the web with the pin, the ladybug would pull forward with all of her strength to break free of that bit of web. As more of the web came off, I saw that some of it was wound around in such a way that it would be impossible for me to help any further without hurting the ladybug.

LADY BUG trapped

In that instant, I realized that it was all a metaphor: that if I tried to do everything for my mother, I could actually hurt her, and even though it's often painful to witness my mother's health challenges, she, like the ladybug, is moving through her struggles using her free will.

LADY BUG free

The ladybug flew off after I realized all of this

160

WHAT inspires you?

Drenched with inspiration
(WHO) inspires us?

Here is a list of some of the people who inspire me. I encourage you to make a similar list. One of my dreams is that each community would have an "inspiration book" like a phone book, with photos and stories about inspiring people. Wouldn't it be wonder-full to page through such a book?

Succulente Americane

Jennifer Wright

Quit her corporate job and learned to teach english as a second language. She now lives and works in the tiny town of Lucca in italy, and rides her bike gleefully around the medieval city. Jennifer is a profoundly endearing person.

Vanessa Carlisle

Co-authored her first book
I was my mother's bridesmaid at age 19, graduated from Reed college with a b.a. in psychology, and worked at a camp that honors kids who just want to lie around and read books. She led nocturnal "dream walks" there. Vanessa is a vibrant adventurer who is effervescently writing and drinking life FULLY.

SABRINA WARD HARRISON

SHE HAS CREATED/WRITTEN 2 BOOKS: Spilling open and Brave on the Rocks. Her compelling Art and spirit Are illuminating souls daily. She is an emotional pioneer who is TAKING exquisite care of Her very own soul. WWW.SABRINAWARDHARRISON.com

Luke Wallis

The First Time I Met Him, He took My Hand and said, "Let's Pray together." When THAT comes From THE HEART of A 2·YEAR·OLD, it's DEEPLY touching. Luke's spirit is uncontainably rich. He is A short warrior with A wise heart.

Nikki and JAY

Nikki teaches unconditional loving Through yoga and "power of one" workshops. She is creating sacred retreat space and studying with shamans From THE AMAZON. Her energy is CALMLY electric.

JAY is A HUGE·HEARTED Musician/scientist who weaves MAGIC in MIND/BODY THROUGH LAUGHTER and sound and is Linking HUMor and Healing In communities nationwide. JAY is an incandescent scoop of Love. TOUCHnHEAL@AOL.com

I AM inspired DAILY By My Friends and neighbors. There Are so Many ways THAT people can inspire US:

Tiny and LARGE Kindnesses, TruTHs toLD, TransformATions, SHAring resources, offering Assistance.

I'm inspired By Conscious pArenting, committed tEACHing, Giving of time and energy, SHAring of DreAMS.

THe More you welcome inspiring people, THe More THey will AppeAr. We Are surrounded By GiFted, inspiring souls. invite some into your Life.

on my WALK, I MeT HAL+ suzanne sHe wore A Crown of Flowers and THeir exuberanT LAuGHter Filled rHe niGHt Air

We went To My House for evening teA...

use Photos, Drawings, parts of letters...
WHO inspires you?

Discovery System
for
inspiration

How Are you inspiring?

What ways do you inspire yourself?

Where and when can you experience inspiration?

reminders:

- encourage and issue unusual invitations
- inspiration can show up suddenly
- welcome inspiring messengers
- list and honor inspiring people and animals in your life
- make a list of treasures
- inspiration loves us to visit it

additional reminders or questions

new views:

- you are already inspiring
- you can become even more inspiring
- our friends are thrilled to be a part of inspiring activities
- sharing inspiration multiplies it
- our "ordinary lives" are full of inspiration
- the more you experience inspiration, the more you will see it

may your life tilt sideways from so much inspiration

Books + resources
inspiration

"everyday when I wake up, I
have a cup of coffee, a sip of
whiskey and a twinkie, and then
I go back to bed."
                        117-year-old woman

12 secrets of Highly Creative women
                        Gail McMeekin

Little Retreats
            Jane Tidbury

FruitFlesh   Gayle Brandeis

Procrastination Handbook
                rita emmett

Little Book of letting Go
            Hugh Prather

Ten Poems to change your Life
                Roger Housden

415·546·3742 (SARK's inspiration Phone Line)
www.andreaScher.com

"I Arise in the morning,
Torn Between a desire to improve
The world and a desire to
enjoy The world. This makes
it Hard to plan the day."
                        E. B. White

TEACHERS

Cheri Huber

Cheri is a Zen meditation teacher and student.

When I found out a number of years ago that I would be meeting her, I got very worried.

My thoughts went like this:

"Oh no! She'll be able to tell that I'm not meditating regularly."

"Oh no! She'll try to get me to meditate regularly."

"I won't be 'Zen enough' for her."

I sat with my agent and friend Debra, and Cheri came rushing toward us, exclaiming:

"I just got back from my trip and this person's child acted like such a brat!"

She flung herself into the chair, laughing.

I instantly relaxed as I witnessed Her crabbiness and impatience.

As I explored Her many books, I learned even more about How to weave one's life out of (everything) that Happens.

another time, CHeri and I saw each other at a cafe in carmel, california. We began discussing why we HADnt called each other. She blurted out,

"you're this big-time famous author! you probably wouldn't have any time for me."

I practically shouted,

"WHAT! you're this acclaimed meditation teacher who will judge me for not meditating and try to lure me to your retreat center!"

We both practically shrieked with laughter and took out our datebooks to exchange numbers.

our
DATe
Books
Bonded!

As I peered into cheri's DATeBook,
I noticed that The writing in it was
very tiny and very meticulous, and
inside very narrow Lines.

Green Gulch
Thunderbird
Drum Dancing
Dog Training
Dalai Lama

I took out my purple
pen and started to write my name and
number, and then suddenly
veered outside The lines, All
THe WAY DOWN THe PAGe! I Heard
Cheri GASp. (i couldn't Help it)

LATer she said,

"Thank you For Helping me to
Get rid of some of THAT

Zen Tenseness!"

Cheri starts Her retreats at 7 Am.
instead of The More common 4 or 5 A.m.
She said,

"They can All wake up THAT early,
I want to sleep!"

i'm waiting For The nocturnal retreat center

Cheri's books are some of the finest tools for awakening that I've discovered. They're simple and deep simultaneously.

She recently came to my house for evening tea, and we shared "deep talk" way into the night... as well as abundant laughter!

Cheri spoke of her special projects:

· A retreat center in Zimbabwe, to assist the young children caring for their younger siblings with AIDS.

· Her book There is nothing wrong with you being released for teens.

· A theme park called "Africa Around the World," which would pay tribute to African culture through the centuries, and educate in a spectacularly fun way.

Cheri teaches at the Zen Monastery Practice Center, and can be reached in the following ways:

Call & Fax: 209·728·3537

e·Mail: zen@mlode.com

Web site: www.cherihuber.com

LucHina Fisher

I First Met LucHina with Her Friend SHarony at a CHicago restaurant. We HAD All Been togetHer at A SARK Book GatHering, and were Feeling very Festive.

I Felt inspired to order A wHole CHocolate caKe for Dessert, and SAiD to THe WAiter,

"Please serve it with no silverware."

We leaned Forward and ate it with no HanDs! As we LAugHeD with our cHocolate-Filled FAces, THe WAiter AsKeD if He coulD try it...

LAter The ManaGer came over and AsKeD to Be included!

riGHt Before we leaned in...

cHocolate soirée

LUCHINA is VIVACIOUS, FUNNY and very TALENTED. SHE HAS just completed A FILM ABOUT THE Life of GLADYS KNIGHT and HAS BEEN A contributing editor AT O MAGAZINE and MANY OTHER PUBLICATIONS.

EVERY TIME I MEET HER FOR DINNER, MY HEART IS FULL and MY SMILE is wide.
AND WE LAUGH WILDLY

LUCHINA CAME TO SAN FRANCISCO TO MAKE A DOCUMENTARY FILM ABOUT HER BROTHER GARY, WHO WAS A writer and DIED of AIDS. THE FILM is A WORK in PROGRESS. SHE MOVED ACROSS THE COUNTRY WITH FEW POSSESSIONS, NO JOB and JUST A little SAVINGS. SHE TOLD ME,

"I never FELT richer or MORE FREE."

THEN SHE TOOK another LEAP OF FAITH and MOVED TO NEW YORK in THE SAME FASHION. THIS TIME, SHE RAN INTO OPRAH'S BEST FRIEND, GAYLE KING, and LEARNED THAT OPRAH WANTED TO SPEAK WITH HER ABOUT A JOB AT THE MAGAZINE, WHICH SHE THEN TOOK.

LUCHINA is Developing other projects for television and writing. She says,

"I feel very prosperous in talent and in love. I didn't ever know my life could be this full!"

Recently, her love, DAVID PARR, surprised her with a visit to a favorite jewelry store where he arranged to have a certain song special to both of them, playing as they walked in. LUCHINA said,

"Listen! Isn't it serendipitous that that music is playing!" (A song by LISA Stansfield called "All Around the world")

He steered her to a jewelry case with a necklace Displayed, and urged her to try it on.

She leaned closer to read the tag and it said,

He then asked her to marry him.

She said yes.

I've been around the world and I, I, I, have found my baby! My sweet LUCHINA I love you with all my heart I want to be with you forever will you...

of course, DAVID HAD Arranged for the Music to be playing (The line on the tag is from that song)

175

leslie Bruhn

leslie is A C.P.A.

Certified Public Accountant,
or Creative Present Accountant

She is Also cofounder of A new Business called Centerfor, which Teaches People About Money and Life in innovative ways. For example, classes on Money Are Taught in A Living room environment with TV trays and nourishing snacks.   Yum!

leslie is Also what I would Describe As A "Gentle C.P.A." She Speaks Softly and Thoughtfully About Money and How it relates to our Lives.

When I First Met with Her, She Said "The word 'Budget' isn't Working For you. Let's just call it A plan."

i instantly Felt relieved

SHE TAUGHT ME THAT "CASH FLOW" IS A CREATIVE ACT. THAT NUMBERS ARE NOT ONLY BLACK AND WHITE, BUT MULTI-COLORED.

I never FELT Judged or ASHAMED with leslie About money, even though I've MADE Many MistAKes and HAD Many Hiding places. SHe Assisted and encouraged Me THROUGH THE process of restructuring My company, CAMP SARK.

Leslie is an integral part of my money TEAM, Along with Irving Bernstein, C.P.A. (who I call the money BUDDHA) and TAMMi, My Bookkeeper (who is refreshingly professional).

Leslie inspires Me About money and AwAkens new AreAs of prosperity. SHe is A COACH, Mentor and teacher. I've learned A lot About DeMystifying money and How it moves (and bets stuck!).

HAving leslie As one of My money Mentors HAs solidified Many of My money practices.

I AM SO GrAte·Full for leslie!

www.center-for.com

Rob practicing "reverse panhandling" to give money away, it took him almost an hour to give away $36 in small bills because people wouldn't take the money!

Rob Brezsny

Rob is an eccentric Poet-Astrologer-Philosopher and Highly Creative Soul. He is a Musician and wrote a novel called The Televisionary Oracle.

His column, "Freewill Astrology," appears in Hundreds of Papers Around the World. He and His editor, Gretchen Giles, have built a Fantastic internet community of like and unlike-minded souls.

www.FreewillAstrology.com

1.900.903.2500 Astrology + more

The only 900 # I recommend and totally worth the money

I FirsT reAD RoB's work in THE early '90s WHen I WAS JUST emerging From my starving Artist DAys. I connected with His rebellious nature and poetic soul.

We HAD endorsed eACH OTHer's BooKs. ADMired eACH OTHer's work, BUT HAD never MeT. So I proposed A "serendipitous encounter" instead of an interview. My idea WAS A silent interview with sKetch Books and pens. *Silence* Born of Fullness

So I went to His House on A clear, CHilly night in OCTober.

As usual with Directions, I WAS slightly Befuddled, and it WAS quite DArk. So I stopped My CAr and Asked THe universe for A sign.

A Deer walked calmly out of some Bushes and toward My CAr. I swear THAT I Heard it say,

"Third House on THe Left."

The Deer was standing About A Foot From me As it "spoke" These words.

W H A T   A   D e e r

I THanked THe Deer, and it WALKed AWAY. THird Hovse on THe lefT, I SAW a man stending in THe DriveWAY, Lit From BeHind. All I Could see WAS WiLD HAir and Some kind of roBe in SilHovette. I Blurted out, "A Deer JusT TALked to Me." RoB AMvsedly SAid,

"Yes, THAT Deer HAS Been Hanging Arovnd lately."

It WOULD TAke A WHole BOOK to recount Our conversaTion. CinnAMon GrAHAM CrAckers and Apples were served. His DAVGHter's Art and Poetry Hangs on THe WAlls.

Here Are A Few ScriBBLings From our Time THAT niGHT:

AvDiBle PrAyers

HOW DO I SEDUCE MY GIRLFRIEND THE GODDESS INTO PROVIDING ME WITH AN ONGOING SERIES OF TENDER LOVING SHOCKS TO KEEP ME WAKING UP AND WAKING UP AND WAKING UP AGAIN?

Gestures of PrAyer

SHekiNAH   Sweet connection To THe Divine

Discovery System for Teachers

Who teaches you?

Who do you teach?

What additional teachers would benefit you?

reminders:

- our learning is activated by exposing ourselves to different teachers
- teachers and students switch places all the time
- teaching expands with what we bring to it
- teaching can occur in unexpected ways

Additional reminders or questions

new views:

- your life is a teaching
- the highest type of teaching is transpersonal
- there are unnamed teachers in your life
- former teachers are still informing your choices
- you are currently a teacher by example

MAY you gleefully be both teacher and student all of your life

Books + resources
Teachers

"There's no use having a universe, a cosmology, if you don't have witnesses. We are the witnesses to the miracle. We're here to be the audience to the magnificent. It is our job to celebrate"
   Ray Bradbury

PEACE PILGRIM
   PEACE PILGRIM

THE DARK side of THE LIGHT CHASERS
   Debbie Ford

Free PLAY
   Stephen Nachmanovitch

Life SKills
   redford williams, M.D.
   Virginia williams, PH.D.

The Feeling Good Handbook
   David Burns, M.D.

Attitudes of Gratitude
   M.J. ryan

301.762.6061 (Dr. Christiane Northrup's Wisdom Wire)
www.oxygen.com

"Don't expect faith
To clear things up for
you. It is Trust, not certainty"

   Flannery O'Connor

Adventures
Adventure Map

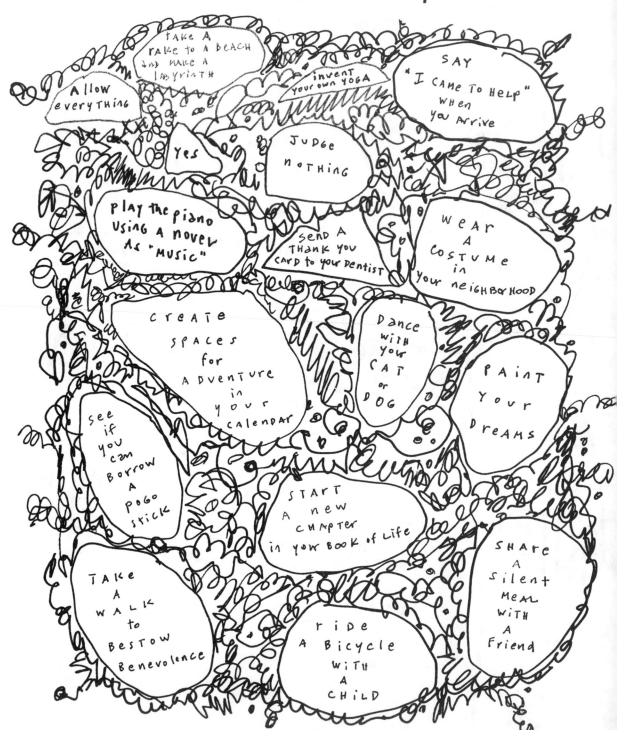

Places of Adventure

One of the best ways to experience prosperity regardless of how much you "have" or "don't have" is to have Plenty of Adventures.

"A small sweet world of
   wave-encompassed wonder"

Swinburne

This was written about the Isle of Sark, a tiny island in the Channel islands, halfway between France and England. This island is the last feudal state in the world, ruled by itself. You must arrive by boat, and there are horse-drawn carts and bicycles instead of cars. There are also secret beaches that become temporary homes for wildflowers when the tide is out.

Dear little Flower Faces

I WAS invited to speak at Yale university, and arrived to find potential adventure in the form of brick pathways, walls of ivy and bright-faced students.

My Host said,

"Across the street is the rare book library, which has translucent marble over the windows, which lets light in but doesn't damage the books."

Then he handed me a magnetic key card and showed me how to wave it at any gate for entry.

I opened the guest book in my suite to see famous names inscribed there. It seemed that there was a secret passageway in the wall, near the fireplace.

I conducted a "Master's tea" at the Master's house, and mingled with the vibrantly alert students. We ate cucumber sandwiches and laughed

secret passageway

AT THE AWKWARDNESS OF SOCIAL CONVENTION.
   AFTER MY TALK, MY HOST SAID,
 " THIS IS THE FIRST TIME THAT GOD,
   SPERM AND VIBRATORS HAVE BEEN TALKED
   ABOUT IN THIS ROOM."
I HAD A MIDNIGHT TOUR OF CAMPUS WITH SOME
ENDEARING STUDENTS. WE ATE OREO COOKIES
IN THE SECRET SOCIETY BUILDINGS.
   THEN I WANDERED BENEATH THE MOON,
WAVING MY KEY CARD AT LARGE WROUGHT-
IRON GATES, AND HEARING THEM CLICK OPEN.

A D V E n T U r e s
      Are All Around Us
   We can prepare by Being
   "ADVenTure - reADY" WHICH is
BASICALLY BeinG willinG To put ourselves

in situations where adventure can occur. This can take place throughout our days, during "ordinary life." you may think you're just on a train or a bus, or in a store, but you're actually (poised) for an adventure.

I met Betty on a flight to Minneapolis, and we spoke for 4 hours about women artists, passion, true purpose, value of collaboration, aging, May Sarton, Mary Oliver, the Isle of Sark, another island off the coast of Scotland, story-telling and art making.

She's the same age as my mother, and has created a show about her life called "Waking up," which incorporates music, film, poetry and dance.

We spoke of shadow work, finding pleasure, speaking and teaching, art in the schools, and fighting for artists' rights.

It was a compendium of pleasure and filled me utterly. Thank you Betty!

Fill yourself with adventure!

Adventure Stories

We can be (Filled to Bursting) with Adventures

I read about this:

The human body is about halfway
in size between an atom and a
star.

Also, scientists have discovered that baby stars have the
ability to burp!

When I turned the page, I discovered this:

7 worshippers in India were killed
when an 80-foot-tall stick of incense
fell and crushed them. It was the
largest stick of incense ever erected.

I read stories like these and my mind
spins with details;

WHO · WHERE · WHY

Our lives are made of adventure
and the stories are everywhere.

The adventures can be common
and uncommon, tiny and large. The
telling and sharing of adventure stories
is an adventure itself!

Adventures Are not only Activity. BASed,
we can Have emotional and spiritual
Adventures too.

Sometimes Adventure comes from stretching
ourselves in new ways.

I Am often reluctant and shy, closed
and unwilling to place myself in the path
of Adventure.

Find Adventure in your shy self too

Adventure Doesnt Mind, it will
come anyway.

Share your Adventure stories with
the world — we need them.

we need to Hear
your Adventures

"The time is always now" peter Beard

remember to wait for adventure to appear— it isn't always obvious.

I went with my friends Tanya and Isabel to the floating homes houseboat tour in Sausalito. It was an absurdly hot day, and I was beginning to feel quite crabby indeed. Then Isabel revealed that we would be visiting residents of the houseboat community, Dana and Denise...

Dana stood outside her houseboat with arms flung wide "welcome!!" She then served cold chocolate cake and drinks and spoke of world wide travel. Adventures unfurled. Denise welcomed us into her "tea House" houseboat, where we took turns in her voluptuous hammock.

The day became an adventure

we never know when the adventures will appear

photo of Dana's houseboat by Isabel Collins

Discovery System
for
Adventures

WHAT ADVENTURES HAVE YOU recently HAD?

WHO can you ADVENTURE WITH?

WHERE will you GO TO ADVENTURE?

reminders:

- Adventures can be Tiny or large
- You can extend invitations to others, or yourself, for Adventure
- We Are surrounded by Adventure opportunities
- You can be shy and still have Adventures
- Sharing an Adventure story is an Adventure in itself
- You can be an emotional or spiritual Adventurer

Additional reminders or questions

new views:

- You can place yourself in the path of Adventure
- Adventures are a way to celebrate being Human
- Your Life is an Adventure
- By focusing on Adventures, you will draw them to you
- There are quiet Adventures
- We naturally crave Adventure

May Adventures find you Grinning all through your Life

Books + resources

Adventures

"Throw your dreams into space
like a kite and you do not know
what it will bring back. A new
life, a new friend, a new love,
a new country." — Anaïs Nin

How To Think Like Leonardo
Da Vinci — Michael J. Gelb

Brave on The Rocks
Sabrina Ward Harrison

Life Makeovers
Cheryl Richardson

The Art of Looking
Sideways
Alan Fletcher

www.girlatplay.com
www.lostsoulcompanion.com
www.hayhouse.com

"It does not do to leave
a live dragon out of
your calculations if
you live near him"
J.R.R. Tolkien

Prosperity Pie

REFRESHMENTS

remember:

   You Are The whole Glorious
Pie! Stuffed Full of Luscious
inGredients, BAked to perfection.

YOU LUSCIOUS THING!

   My Friends Giselle and EARL HAD
A "pie PARTY" AT THeir Home. every
Kind of pie WAS represented: SWEET,
SAVOry, MEAT, vegetAble. It WAS Fun
To MATCH THe pies WITH THe people...
   I PAinted A "pie" and wrote A
PrAyer in THe center.

I   SEND   YOU   MY   PrAyer pie

Prayer Pie

MAY YOU UNFOLD WILLINGLY
MAY YOU BE TRULY NOURISHED
MAY PEACE BE IN YOUR EVERY STEP
MAY GRATITUDE FILL YOU
MAY YOU REACH OTHERS WITH YOUR
RADIANT HEART

love, SARK

restorAtions

Prosperity pie Means THe
W Hole   pie:
THe CrinGinG, FraGile pArts of
ourselves, As well As THe SOAYING,
Successful ones. THe Acceptance
of THe unAcceptAble:

   " until we HAVe Become THAT
   WHiCH we Are DemonstratinG
   AGAinsT, we will HAVe MADe no
   ProGress"
                  THicH NHAT HanH

   I HAVe Found THAT Im not As
"GOOD" AS I THOUGHT or As "BAD"
AS I FeAred. I AM not Heroine
or VillAin.
   ⟨ I AM LivinG with My ACTUALself ⟩

   and SeeinG WHAT THAT iS.
   NeiTHer ideALizinG nor BeinG
ideALized.
   It is More pAinFUL THan I
HAD iMAGined.   197

Also more Dimensional.
   I Find myself stumbling
Hand in Hand with Forgiveness
As a much closer entity.
   May you continue To
restore, explore, eat pie,
Fill your Home and Heart
with Laughter, embrace The
Pain, peer into The Darkness

Take Difficult routes
   re-energize yourself,
Continue re-covering and
Dis-covering
      Seeing Fresh

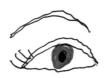

Seeing   Fresh
      means
Accepting everything
Judging nothing

Practice Fiercely

198

reminders

We are all in the process of re-covering and dis-covering ourselves. We discover our faults, weaknesses, joys and hopes.

We re-cover what's been lost, hidden, obscured, blocked or diverted.

This is our communion, our shared journey.

It is full of false starts, detours, obstructions, mis-directions, repeats, rare finds, states of grace, moments of synchronicity and serendipitous encounters.

There is no reason for it to get easier.

There (is) reason for us to get easier, looser, softer, more

receptive.

HOW can we Allow THE UNTHINKABLE? HOW Can we expand our Definitions to include THE ACTUALITY of it All?

We Are often so BUSY Dividing it All up into GOOD/BAD MAD/SAD lost/Found.

WHAT if we Blur THE SHARP Divides and SMEAR it All together? It WOULD BE A Marvelous Tapestry I AM sure.

Discovery System
for
Prosperity Pie

WHAT'S in your pie?

How Do you refresh yourself?

WHO SURROUNDS you WITH LOVE?

201

reminders:

- We Are All in The process of Discovery and recovery
- THere is no reason For Life to Get easier
- THere is reason for us To Get easier
- widen your FIELD of Acceptance
- You Are THe WHole pie
- THe WHole pie includes All THe pAin As well As THe positive
- See FresH

Additional reminders & Questions

new views:

- prosperity pie is not related to Amounts of Money or possessions
- pie is MADe To Be SHAred
- you can cHoose to relAx About Money and everyTHing else
- prosperity is A process, not A Destination
- you Are Delicious!

MAY you Be constantly Filled So you MAY Fill oTHers

Books + resources
Prosperity pie

" Be very careful about locating
good or God, right or wrong,
legal or illegal, at your favorite
level of consciousness "
                    Timothy Leary

The Dance
        Oriah Mountain Dreamer

A Little More About Me
            Pam Houston

How to Get From Where
You Are To Where You Want
To Be   Cheri Huber

Stretching Lessons
            Sue Bender

www.networkforgood.org

" The soul needs regression
as much as it needs
evolution, development
and progress "
            Thomas Moore

It is essential THAT We eACH
Develop our inner prosperity, So THAT
We can Be of GREATer service To ourselves
aND THe WorLD. our FullNess can HeLP
To Fill anoTHer's emptiNess.

We can THen stand FuLLy TOGeTHer
As THe WorLD SHiFTs and CHanGes.
no MATter WHAT THose chanGes Are

Bless Us All in THese terrible anD
TenDer Times. Let us see THe opportunities
for HeALinG everyWHere we look. See love

BAke your Prosperity pie with
GreAT LOVe, SHare THe pieces From A
Sense of plenty. Let's WAKe up even
MOre, Brin6 FresH enerGy anD New
PermissioN To THis WiLD, Precious,
ACHinG, DiVine experience caLLeD
LiFe.

Let's DRAW BranD-New pictures of
Prosperity anD expanD our ABiLiTy To
Transcend and transforM.

I'll Be riGHT Here, GrowinG anD
leArninG AlonG with you.

All THe LoVe in THe WorLD
SARK San Francisco OCToBer 2001

Pie Power

ABOUT CAMP SARK

WEB. SiGHT: WWW. CAMPSARK. COM
for MORE ABOUT SARK., ordering HER BOOKS
and MORE AT THE MAGIC COttAGEstore, or to "lunGe+CHAT"

e. MAiL: CAMPSARK@CAMPSARK·COM
CALL : 4 15. 397·7275 information line
spells sark

SPEAKING
enGAGements: see "SPEAKING enGAGements on WeB· SiGHT
or e. MAiL anne@CAMPSARK.com

CALL THE inspiration Line (celebrating its 10th anniversary!)
415. 546·3742 (epic) 24 HOURS "A PLACE TO Be How You ActuALLy Are"

resource PAGes

To order:
Succulent WILD WoMan
THE BODACIOUS BOOK of Succulence
Change Your Life Without Getting out of BED
Transformation Soup
EAT MANGOES NAKED or for More copies of Prosperity Pie

CALL: 1.800.223.2336 Simon & Schuster
FAX: 1.800.943.9831
Write: 100 Front ST. riverside, New Jersey 0 8075
WeB: WWW.SiMONSAYS.COM
CALL: Special sales for special-discounts for
Groups + Teachers 1.800.456.6798

To order:
A Creative Companion
inspiration Sandwich
SARK's Journal & PLay! BOOK
LIVING JUICY
THE MAGIC Cottage ADDress BOOK
CALL: 1.800.841.2665 Celestial
(BOOK)   ARTS
WeB: www.tenspeed.Com

WE ALL love BOOKS!

Pie Professionals

THANKS So MUCH For All THE professionals
THAT contribute to My work, and To THIS WORLD
THank YOU!

- TO MY COMPANY, CAMP SARK, 9 YEARS OLD, and to All THose WHo Assist in its GroWTH
- TO MY PUBLISHER, SiMON & SCHUSTER
- To MY Assistant, anne FerGuson: A remarkably efficient and visionary virtual Assistant, and To THose WHo Assist Her: MARK, JAKUB, eileen
- To MY CreATive Book production Assistant, andreA Scher: an exceptionally TAlented and luminous Assistant who works Buoyantly and BeAutifully
- To MY incredible MoNey teAM: irving Bernstein C.P.A., leslie Bruhn C.P.A, TAMMi reidl/Bookkeeper, LINDA Lippstreu/Banker, June DAvid/MortgAge Broker
- To MY Gifted AGents, DeBrA Goldstein, MARY ann nAples, THe creative culture
- To MY Brilliant Business COACH, PATriciA Huntington
- To MY Awesome Attorney, lArry rosenthal + For Business ADvising
- To (All) MY Fellow AuTHors, incluDing: Cheri Huber, MAYA anGelou, Joan Borysenko, Lou PAGes, oriAH Mountain Dreamer, SABrinA WARD HArrison, MAGGie oHman SitHAnnon, roByn posin, For kindred spiritship + support. A speciAl THank You to Cheryl richardson for MentoriNG + vision + invitations of prosperity
- To THe FABulous FilM Folks: CHARTHoUse, oXYGen, ZolAr entertAinment
- To stACY Brice of Assist U For providing Such service and introduction to anne Ferguson, virtuAl Assistance is Astounding! WWW.Assistu.com
- To THe remarkable KAY DAVi for Business MentoriNG
- To MY HeALTH CAre teAM: leo, Joe, PATriciA, VADan, YoFe, BAY club, elson HAAS
- To MY committed travel Agent: HolGer
- To THe Divine DiAne reHM and Her teAM AT NPr
- To Dr. Jenny TAYlor for Feline wisdom and Penelope SMith for telepATHic support
- To THe PUBlisHer of MY First 5 Books, CelestiAl ARts
- To FeMAil CreAtions, iMPACt, Cedco, RUG BArn, portAl, CHARTHouse, licensing PArtners
- To MY FormeR Business PArtners: BriGette ScHeel and ADrienne steele, WHo Helped To set so MAny projects into Motion

   SpeciAl THanks To THe United sHuttle and Bill clinton!

THank YOU All

GLitter · Pie People

if you are reading This, YOU Are one of THeSe PeoPLe!
THank you For welcoming My ART and Words

YOU GLOW

To My MoM, MArvelous MArjorie and Her Friends and supporters: CATHY + MARC, BoB, Dick + MArilyn, PATTY lee, Meg + MArk, KATHLeen, PASTor AHL, Doris + MArcia, PHyllis *i love you*

THANK YOU

Andrew/SuPerB BroTHer + TanyA/Dear Soul + Ben/Dear DoG, 2ndreA/endearing Button

BiBBo/Deluxe DreamBoAT + Judy + silvana Bill + MAY-Ree/Beloved Cousins + cHellie + Kim, Jim + sally Bill HuBner/Gorgeous moments **C**raig McNair Wilson/incandescent Soul ClAire NorTH/irish love ChelseA/Whose 6 year old self Healed me CHeri HuBer/zen Humor Debbie edwards/Divine spirit DeBrA + Steven/Lusciously **D**e LiSSA/SuBLime Friend + Alex + cHarlie *cat love* +BoDHi eleanor/Juicy FruiT eMily ClAire/Beloved niece + GoD cHiLD **G**ary rosenTHAL/Deep Poet

HoLY **i**SABeL Collins/MAjestic WomAn illana/Songs of THe Soul ilene Cummings/Treasure HEART iSABeL THe younger **J**uPiter/SHeer Love JoHn + robin/Succulently Jan + MArcus + MArina/My Adopted MPLS FAMILY *Bless you* Jen-Jen/AdoringLY Joshua + nick/rumi Flute Jude +JoHn/Dearly JoHn + Lois/sweeTLY Joe Brown/ "A raccoon touched me!" **K**ATHryn + AjA/ serendiPitously Karen Drucker/new sister song Katie + ToPHer/engagingly **L**arry/indeliBle support + love Luchina + David/ I, I, I Leigh/Awareness **M**ike + jill/Deep comFort Mike roBBins/endearingLY MAry ann + TiM/radiantLY **N**ikki + JAY/Life as Music Nicole young + kids/Adventure FAMILY neigHBors: SALLY, MicHAeL, JoHn + lea, Judy, speedys, WILD Parrots **P**ATriciA + Brandy/Teacher of LigHT + F.Y.L.U.Y.B.H **R**AY DAVi/wiTH Love roy Carlisle/FATHer of Vanessa roByn Posin/rare Bird **S**ABrina + SAM/Conscious connection and Best "BASic" Susan BeArdsley/Deep TALK + DreAms of AFricA Suzi rendall/sPLendid LaugHTer Suzanne + Denoon/Grinning Stella/SPirited **T**ori/TruLY Todd/BrigHTness **V**anessA/GiFTed writer-woman Virginia Bell/Clear cHannel ViMALA/Fierce TruTH **Y**oFe/Swim sister, Aries/scorPio Moon **Z**oe/Adored GoDcHILD SPeciAL TriBuTe To My new counTry of ireLaND! THank you To MirAVAL, YALe university, BenjAMin HoTeL and San Francisco

Be an eMoTional Pioneer